FIRST TIME

FIRST TIME SELLER

Also available

Getting the Builders in
The Right Way to Write Your Own CV
Wedding Etiquette Properly Explained
Best Man's Duties

FIRST TIME
BUYER
FIRST TIME
SELLER

Get *Your* Foot on the Property Ladder

Paul Jager

RIGHT WAY

Typeset in 10pt Times by Letterpart Ltd., Reigate, Surrey.
Printed and bound in Great Britain by Cox & Wyman Ltd.,
Reading, Berkshire.

The *Right Way* series is published by Elliot Right Way Books,
Brighton Road, Lower Kingswood, Tadworth, Surrey, KT20 6TD,
U.K. For information about our company and the other books we
publish, visit our website at www.right-way.co.uk

Dedication

To my Mother and Father for all their support
and Susan Lehmann for her guidance and proof
reading skills

Acknowledgements

Anthony Bell, Christopher Long, Shashi Rathod,
Steve Cornish

CONTENTS

Part III: Buying and Selling Property: The Final Step

INTRODUCTION

Tullulah Bankhead, the famous Hollywood actress, once said

> "If I had to live my life again, I'd make exactly the same mistakes ... only sooner."

If only it were possible to make all our mistakes early in life. We can, though, learn from the mistakes of others, instead of committing them ourselves. This is the goal of 'First Time Buyer: First Time Seller'; to avoid the pitfalls that others have faced when buying or selling property for the first time.

With the author's years of experience in the estate agency profession, he gives the reader the insider's perspective on all the tips and tricks.

As the title suggests, the book is divided into two parts. The first tackles the subject from the purchaser's viewpoint. You'll discover how to navigate the property maze expertly, and:

- Find your perfect home

- Successfully negotiate a sale

- Organise the mortgage and solicitor

- Confidently resolve common problems.

The second half of the book is written for those selling property, although it is also an important read for the first time buyer, who needs to understand how the seller sees things. It reveals how to:

- Choose the right estate agent

- Prepare your home for marketing

- Deal with offers like a professional

- Take control of your sale through to its successful conclusion.

Common to both parts of the book are sections entitled 'The Problem Clinic'. These identify common dilemmas that face buyers and sellers, and offer suggestions to resolve them.

So, without wasting any more time, our journey begins ...[1]

---

[1] In the same way that the hu*man* race includes both men and women, the words 'he' or 'his' refer to both the male and female gender. No disrespect to the ladies is intended, and it makes the book read much better!

It should also be noted that this book discusses procedures and legal matters employed in England and Wales, Scotland having its own method of buying and selling property.

PART I
FIRST TIME BUYER

1

PREPARATION

The key to success when buying a property for the first time is preparation. This is a principal theme of the book.

The journey ahead of us needs thorough planning, and involves asking three basic but vital questions:

- How strong is my desire to buy?

- What type of home do I need?

- What can I afford?

How Strong is My Desire to Buy?

Is the need to buy a property a definite one? At this early stage, indecision is not a problem. Asking yourself this question later, after a vendor has accepted your offer, will not be appreciated. If the purchasers are a couple, are *both* committed to ownership? Is the relationship secure enough to warrant buying a home together, which is 'life changing', not to mention expensive.

What Type of Home Do I Need?

Start by listing the features your new home will require. Don't think only of your present needs, but consider the next twelve to twenty four months. Take time to consider this. Ask friends and family for advice.

- Price – first time buyers with a tight budget will need to consider carefully how much can be comfortably spent on a property

- What accommodation is required? For those on a tight budget (as most first time buyers are), the accommodation on offer will be limited. Properties at the lower end of the market will probably consist of little more than a lounge, bathroom/WC, kitchen and bedroom(s), with the possibility of a garden area. Studio flats are even more compact, combining the lounge, kitchen and bedroom together in one single area

- Is it necessary to be near shops and transport? Location is an important consideration; and the old estate agency saying is true: 'It is better to have the worst property in the best area than the best property in the worst area.' It is easier to improve a property than it is an area

- Town or country? Living in the country may be a wonderful dream but is it practical?

- Houses are often more expensive than flats. Would it be better to buy a higher quality and larger apartment than a comparably priced but smaller house?

- What parking facilities are required? (Garages are very useful for all that junk that parents refuse to store!)

- Planning for a family? Will a flat be large enough? Will schooling be an issue?

- Is it appropriate to buy a newly built home? Initially, they require less maintenance than an older type of property. However, you may pay a premium for 'buying new'. Remember, that sparkling kitchen and beautiful bathroom will soon look worn and used

- To help with the mortgage payments, would it be wise to buy a property with one more bedroom than you need? It can then be rented out and provide additional household income (this may involve tax and mortgage implications which need to checked)

- Is there the time, energy, and resources to look after a house, or would a flat be more appropriate? On the page opposite we look at the pros and cons of each:

HOUSES

Houses are normally built over two floors and the commonest are:

- *Terraced*: a row of properties attached to each other

- *Semi-detached*: houses which are built in pairs

- *Detached*: a property standing apart from others

- *Townhouse*: the accommodation for this type of home is arranged differently from any of those defined above. It is usually built over three floors; with the lounge on the first floor, while the bedrooms are often divided over the first and second floors. The garage can be an integral part of the building, or be in a separate garage block

- *Bungalow*: while not strictly a house, it only differs by being constructed on a single floor.

Houses are normally freehold, unlike flats which are usually leasehold, so the purchaser owns the property without any timescale restrictions or imposed maintenance charges.

Advantages of buying a house compared to a flat:

- Greater privacy and own garden

- Possibly less noise

- Own front door rather than a communal entrance

- Possibly larger accommodation

- The opportunity to extend and alter the property in the future (subject to any restrictions).

Disadvantages of buying a house, compared to a flat:

- Generally more expensive to maintain and heat (because it has more than one floor)

- Possibly more expensive to buy.

FLATS

Flats and maisonettes are a popular choice for the first time
buyer. They can be purpose built (which means constructed for
that purpose) or converted (a building which has later been
changed into flats).

Although the terms 'flat' and 'maisonette' are often used
interchangeably, there are strictly speaking differences between
the two:

- Flats are usually one of many in a block, maisonettes can
  form part of a smaller building.

- Unlike a maisonette, a flat has a communal entrance
  before reaching its front door.

- A maisonette may have its own garden area, while a flat's
  tends to be communal (if it has any), i.e. for the benefit of
  all the residents.

For simplicity, the remainder of the book will use the term 'flat'
to describe both types.

IS A FLAT FOR ME?

For some, living in a flat is ideal.

- Those with busy lifestyles benefit from occupying a building where the maintenance is undertaken by others (the
  managing agent or residents' association).
    This generally includes communal gardens, repairs to
  the building, and external decoration.

- There is a greater feeling of security being in close proximity to others. This, though, can be a disadvantage, if noise
  becomes an issue.

Disadvantages include:

- Climbing flights of stairs.

- Restrictions in the lease which might, for example, prohibit
  pets or the erection of a satellite dish.

Compared with houses, there are three additional matters to consider with a flat:

Costs. There may be additional expenditure i.e. ground rent, and maintenance (often called service) charge. Buyers need to allow for these in their living expenses, and be aware of any potential for changes to them in the future.

The ground rent is usually a nominal amount, payable to the freeholder e.g. £100 per year.

The maintenance charge, which is more applicable to flats than maisonettes, is paid towards the upkeep of the building. It can vary greatly from block to block, depending on how well they are cared for. Lifts for example are an expensive luxury, and can greatly increase the maintenance charge. Confirm that no costly repairs to the building are imminent, as you will be expected to contribute; a nasty shock if you have only recently moved in!

Which Floor? Consider the pros and cons of living on particular floors of a block. The ground floor may be more of a security risk than higher floors. However, stairs are an inconvenience when you are weighed down with shopping bags or a pushchair. This is why first floor flats are so popular; fewer stairs to climb, and less chance of a burglar shinning up a drainpipe to your window.

The Lease. Flats and maisonettes are normally leasehold properties. This means that the owner of the building (the freeholder) grants the buyer exclusive possession of the flat for an agreed period. This is detailed in the lease, a document that also defines

a)   your responsibilities as the 'owner', and

b)   who has responsibility for other aspects of the building e.g. maintenance such as the gardens, internal and external decoration, common areas such as halls, landings and stairways, the roof, and window cleaning etc. This is either under the supervision of the residents' association or a third party called a 'managing agent'.

It is possible to purchase a flat, which in addition to the lease also has its share of the building's freehold. If the residents have ownership of the freehold, the advantages are:

●   The duration of the leases can be extended for little charge.

- There may be little point in paying ground rent, as the party receiving it are the residents.

- It is a nice 'extra' to offer when reselling the property.

- The residents have greater control over the building.

What Can I Afford?
Most first time buyers need financial help to buy a property. This is normally in the form of a mortgage, from a bank/ building society or through an independent financial adviser. While the first offer their own specific mortgage products, the latter can recommend mortgages from many different sources.

Searching for the right mortgage can be a dizzying experience. There are so many types to choose from. They seem to change constantly. There is so much jargon to learn. Once again, a little time spent preparing will help you through this maze. Begin by asking:

- Can I afford the monthly mortgage payments? This is a long-term commitment, and a regular income and strict budget plan will be needed. A financial adviser will ask that a 'Client Fact Find' form be completed to help answer this question.

- Is it appropriate to buy a home? Are your personal and financial circumstances secure enough for such a major commitment?

- Can the costs involved in running a home be met? This includes utility bills, credit card payments, food, clothes, recreation, council tax, telephone bills, inevitable repairs, building and contents insurance, travel and car expenses, and general maintenance.

THE MORTGAGE AMOUNT
The next step is to decide on the amount of mortgage to be borrowed. This is often based on the buyer's means. For example, an individual earning £30,000 a year, and able to obtain a mortgage equal to 2.5 times his income, would be offered £75,000. A couple, who are both salaried, could be given a mortgage of three times their joint income. Each lender

has its own criteria. Overtime, bonuses, and existing financial commitments may factor into the calculation in varying ways.

The amount of mortgage payable each month depends on

● The sum borrowed.

● The interest rate associated with the mortgage. This is the cost of borrowing that money. For example, a £50,000 mortgage with a 4% interest rate will be a more expensive proposition than a £50,000 mortgage at 3.5% interest.

● The sum borrowed compared to the value of the property. A mortgage company takes a risk each time it lends money for a property. This risk increases the greater the amount lent compared to the value of the property. For example a mortgage of £50,000 on a property worth £100,000 is a relatively small risk. If the monthly mortgage payments cease the lender is still likely to recover its £50,000. However, lend £95,000 on a property worth £100,000 (95% mortgage) and the chance of recovering this amount, if the property market falters and the building decreases in price, is smaller. To counter this greater risk, higher percentage loans may bring with them higher interest rates.

● The length of the mortgage. The normal term for a mortgage is 25 years, but for a longer period the monthly payments will be lower (although the amount paid overall will be higher).

In times of low interest rates, mortgage companies are keen to lend money. But, 'what goes down must go up'. If a mortgage of £100,000 at a 3.5% interest rate is affordable at one time, could the repayments still be managed if interest rates rose to 5%, 6% or higher? This must be considered. To give an idea of the scale of the problem, here are the monthly payments on a straightforward repayment mortgage of £100,000 over 25 years:

4%	£527.84
5%	£584.59
6%	£644.30
7%	£706.78
8%	£771.82

And they can go higher than that! In the late 1980s mortgage rates reached 15%, which would put the repayment on the same basis up to £1280.83.

MORTGAGE TYPES
There is a range of mortgages available, the most typical include

- Repayment mortgage – each month a portion of the loan and the interest on that loan is paid. These result in the loan being paid off by the end of the mortgage term.

- Interest only mortgage – each month only the interest on the sum borrowed is paid; the actual amount of mortgage remains constant throughout the term of the loan. The latter is repaid by putting money each month into an investment plan. Although the overall monthly payments may be less than those for a repayment mortgage, there is a risk that the investment will not provide enough to pay off the mortgage at the end. Therefore, a regular review is necessary (on the bright side, it is also possible that this investment might grow quicker than expected and help pay the mortgage off early). The investment plan can be an endowment, personal pension plan, or ISA (individual savings account). Advice is needed as to which is the most suitable for your own personal circumstances.

There are at least five options as to how the interest rates may be calculated.

Variable Rate. The interest rate on the mortgage can go up and down.

Fixed Rate. The interest rate is fixed, for an amount of time, making it easier to keep to a budget (particularly useful for first time buyers, who, apart from moving costs, also have the cost of furnishing their new home).

Capped Rate. This is a fusion of variable and fixed rates. The interest rate is variable but will not go above a certain limit, for an agreed period.

Tracker. Tracker mortgages are designed to mirror the movement of the mortgage base rate.

Discount Rate. A discounted rate, based on the lender's variable rate, is offered for a fixed period of time, e.g. 1% off the variable rate for two years.

A lender may also offer a more competitive interest rate if you have a larger deposit. It might also be possible to reduce the initial monthly mortgage payments by starting with an interest only mortgage, and changing to a repayment one after a few years. Having such flexibility is a useful feature. Other questions for a buyer to ask include:

- Will it be possible to pay in lump sums to help reduce the mortgage, and so repay it earlier than expected?

- If times become difficult, will taking a break from mortgage payments be allowed? If so, will any charges apply?

At times when lenders are 'keen' for your business, it is worth shopping around for such facilities.

APR

When mortgage rates are advertised, two figures are quoted, one with the term 'APR'. This stands for Annual Percentage Rate. Required by the 1974 Consumer Credit Act, it is a system used to help make a fairer comparison between the rates of different lenders.

The percentage rate without the 'APR' phrase, is the actual rate of interest payable for that particular mortgage. The APR rate takes into account, for example (a) any other charges associated with taking that mortgage and (b) the way a particular lender calculates its interest payments over the term of the mortgage (because companies can calculate this in a number of ways). Consequently, because the APR rate includes the above, a more informed decision should be possible when judging how competitive a particular mortgage scheme is. However, nothing in life is simple. Organisations can have their own methods of determining APR, depending on the type of mortgage schemes they provide. Therefore it may be advisable to decide on a suitable mortgage by asking a financial adviser to calculate what your actual monthly mortgage payments will be for specific mortgage schemes. Ensure that you also enquire about the costs involved with obtaining that mortgage, such as valuation fees, any additional solicitor's costs, or administration fees.

THE BEST OF TIMES ...THE WORST OF TIMES

What would happen to the mortgage payments if severe illness or unemployment were to strike? Being prepared for such eventualities is a wise precaution. Most mortgage lenders will offer services to allow for these circumstances:

- Illness – sickness can leave an individual unable to work, and without an income (or a greatly reduced one). A 'critical illness' insurance policy may provide a cash lump sum, or monthly payments to help pay the mortgage.

- Death – an insurance policy can be taken to ensure that dependants are not left to cope with a mortgage, if the main provider dies.

- Unemployment – this protects against the loss of employment, and consequently income.

It is imperative to understand the exact coverage of each company's policies before committing to them.

FREEBIES

Before choosing a mortgage lender, ask what 'extras' they are offering. For example, is there free legal advice or solicitor's services? Some might provide a survey at no charge. Is 'cash back' available with any of a company's mortgage schemes? Buying a property is such an expensive proposition that such 'goodies' are hard to ignore. However, ensure that they are not simply camouflage, disguising a mortgage product that in the long term could prove more costly than others.

THE DEPOSIT

Although mortgages for the entire purchase price are available, it is customary to buy a property with a mixture of mortgage and a buyer's own money. The latter is called the 'deposit'. For example, if a mortgage of £90,000 is being borrowed, and the buyer has £10,000 savings, a home of £100,000 can be bought (assuming you have additional money to set aside for other moving expenses e.g. solicitors, stamp duty, removals etc. See below).

Even at this early stage, it is important to confirm that

- The deposit is definitely available, particularly if being provided by family or friends

- There are no delays obtaining the deposit. For example, do shares need to be sold, or is the money being transferred from abroad? This will affect the timescale of any offer you make.

If no deposit is available, then a mortgage for the entire value of the property is required. This is called a '100% mortgage'. However, there is a major disadvantage with this, because the mortgage lender is taking a great risk in providing the full amount of the loan. Imagine the following: mortgage interest rates start to rise. This causes the public to become cautious about buying property and so property prices begin to fall. Now imagine we own a house and bought it with a 100% mortgage. Having never considered that mortgage rates might one day increase, we now find that our income does not cover the new higher monthly mortgage payments. To remedy the situation we decide to sell, but with house prices declining the amount realised now will be less than the value of the 100% loan. In this situation, the company providing the loan for the entire amount of the property would now be showing a loss. To overcome the problem of having no financial commitment from the buyer when taking a 100% mortgage, mortgage lenders will reflect this in their interest rates. These are unlikely to be as competitive as mortgages for a lesser percentage, and will be accompanied by additional costs, an arrangement fee, or an insurance policy in case of non-payment, known as an MIG (Mortgage Indemnity Guarantee to cover the lender). These matters need to be fully investigated before pursuing such a route.

ADDITIONAL COSTS
There is much to consider when buying a first home, so it is easy to overlook other associated expenses.

1. Stamp duty, correctly referred to as stamp duty land tax. This is a government tax, paid by the purchaser once the property has been bought. The amount is dependent on the sale price. (The rates and thresholds given below are correct at the time of going to press, but can be changed by the Chancellor of the Exchequer at any time, so you should check the up-to-date position.)

   Up to and including £60,000 – Nothing payable

   Over £60,000 up to and including £250,000 – 1% of the entire price of the property

   Over £250,000 up to and including £500,000 – 3% of the entire price of the property

   Over £500,000 – 4% of the entire price of the property.

2. Survey fees

3. Land Registry fee (registering the property in the new owner's name)

4. Unexpected costs, e.g. additional surveys if defects are found

5. Removal costs

6. Household items

7. Building insurance (put in place from 'exchange of contracts', to cover the property for damage, fire, subsidence etc). It may be worth enquiring whether there are any incentives for taking building insurance from the same company that is lending you the mortgage.

8. Are penalties incurred if the mortgage is paid off early? Is there a 'booking fee' to take advantage of a particular mortgage scheme?

9. Abortive sale (the buyer or seller decides not to proceed). In this situation, costs already incurred may be lost, such as survey fee, solicitor's fees, and mortgage arrangement fee.

10. Your solicitor at 'exchange of contracts' will need 5%-10% of the purchase price. This is a non-returnable deposit.

11. Solicitors' fee. This is worthy of further explanation. In order to buy a property, ownership needs to be transferred to the purchaser, using legal documents and procedures. This is called 'conveyancing' and is undertaken by a solicitor (or legal executive, or licensed conveyancer). The difference between a solicitor, legal executive and licensed conveyancer is one of experience and qualification. All three are able to deal competently with the conveyancing process, however the solicitor has a broader range of legal knowledge and can therefore deal with any other law related matters, such as wills, while the licensed conveyancer is only qualified to deal with the conveyancing procedure itself. The term 'solicitor' is used for the remainder of the book to denote all three types of conveyancer.

When choosing a solicitor, pick one who has the time and patience to guide you through the process. These are qualities worth paying for (and I would always advocate using a solicitor rather than attempting the legal work yourself).

Their fee is based on either an hourly rate, or a single amount for the entire transaction. Choose two or three solicitors and compare their charges and service before making a decision. Confirm the cost of the 'total' package, whether the fee includes any additional costs (for legal documents such as searches), and if there is a charge for an abortive sale.

Having made your choice, confirm that you want to use their services, and will call again when a property has been found; it is premature to incur any expenses at this stage.

2

LOOKING FOR PROPERTY

The preparation is complete. Now the most exciting part of our journey begins: searching for our dream home.

The Estate Agent

The most popular and successful method of finding properties for sale is through estate agents. Their reputation may have been tarnished over the years, but they still offer the only access to the vast majority of properties for sale in England and Wales.

Competition for property can be fierce with far more people (called 'applicants' or 'buyers') wanting to buy than there are homes for sale. An agent might be marketing 20 flats, but hold information on over 200 flat seekers. It is impossible for the agent to contact all these people simultaneously each time a flat comes to the market. There will always be some who, through chance alone, are lucky enough to be informed first. They now have the opportunity to make an offer before anyone else! However, this limitation of the system can work in the educated buyer's favour.

TAKING ADVANTAGE OF THE SYSTEM

Successful estate agents will always keep a select list of applicants interested in specific types of property. These are people who the agent believes are keen to buy immediately (so bringing him closer to a sale and his monthly commission cheque). They are termed 'hot prospects', and immediately contacted when a suitable property becomes available. How can you become one of this elite number?

- You have already fulfilled the first requirement by following the advice in the previous chapter: being prepared. This demonstrates to the agent that you have taken this matter seriously.

- Prove you are a keen buyer by being enthusiastic and *ready to view properties at every opportunity.*

- Follow the instructions in this chapter!

YOUR VITAL STATISTICS

Leave your property requirements with as many estate agents as possible. Visit rather than telephone (personal contact increases the chance of being remembered).

The agent will start by asking for name, address, and contact details. Leave plenty of these; how unfortunate would it be to miss the ideal property because the agent only had your work telephone number? If the estate agent is technologically savvy he may also be able to email or send a text message, with details of homes for sale.

After noting your price range and property requirements, the agent will then ask three very important questions. The answers will brand you as either 'Mr Average' buyer or a 'hot prospect' worthy of special attention:

- When do you want to buy?

- When can you view?

- Do you have a property to sell?

'Now'
'Now', and
'I am a first time buyer and can purchase a property immediately' is what you tell them, emphatically.

Lastly, they may offer free mortgage advice from the agency's in-house financial adviser. Take advantage of this. There is no obligation, and ideas might be suggested which you hadn't considered before; seize any opportunity to learn from those in the profession.

PROPERTY DETAILS

Having matched your requirements to the agency's properties, you'll be given the appropriate property detail sheets. If, in the past, estate agents were renowned for pushing poetic licence to its limits, the 1991 Property Misdescriptions Act (PMA) now ensures all material has to be factual and honest. No longer does the phrase 'situated within a five minute walk of the shops' mean 'but only for those blessed with the lightning speed of an Olympic sprinter'. Even the photographs have to conform to the PMA and accurately reflect the true nature of a property. If, however, anything remains unclear, ask further questions such as:

- Is the property situated on a main road?

- What lies at the rear of the garden?

- How old is the maisonette?

- How many flats are there in the block?

- If unclear from the photograph, what lies either side of a property?

You may also find that agents supply details on homes in excess of your budget. They assume that

- The owner may consider an offer from a first time buyer, if his aim is to move quickly

- The buyer may pay a little more for the ideal property.

These are reasonable assumptions. A buyer should also remain open-minded when studying the details, as properties that may initially seem unsuitable could be altered to fulfil his needs. For example:

- The spacious flat with panoramic views, but the awful 1960s kitchen and poor decoration. The latter can easily be rectified over time (funds permitting).

- That perfect two-bedroom cottage, which has a through lounge when two rooms were wanted. Could this lounge be partitioned into two (subject to regulations)?

- For a first home, how much of a real disadvantage is it to have a maisonette with an electric heating system instead of a gas one?

Never compromise your standards, just stay aware of a home's potential.

YOUR BEST FRIEND – THE ESTATE AGENT!

To increase the chance of becoming a 'hot prospect', strike up a personal rapport with the estate agent. Agents are accustomed to apathy and defensiveness from the public. Be different. Take an interest in them. They are more likely to do business with someone they like and feel comfortable with, rather than an applicant who treats them like just another salesman. Keep in regular contact so that you are at the forefront of their minds when that beautiful home becomes available.

The Auction Room

Purchasing a property at auction is an option the first time buyer should be wary of. It may be important to question why the owner (or person in charge of the property) has decided to go to auction, rather than use an estate agent. It is possible that the property has a problem, i.e. structural defects or in need of renovation, which would have made a sale on the open market very difficult. This may result in the property being sold at a discounted price, but you must consider how much any work will cost, and how much effort would be required in finding willing tradesmen to complete the work. You must also bear in mind that a lender may not be happy to provide a mortgage on this type of property, with the risks involved.

Clearly, a lot of research must be undertaken before a first time buyer even considers bidding for such a property.

The method of sale at an auction is entirely different from that of an estate agent, although it does initially involve viewing the property for sale.

- The 'offer' is made in an auction room, in the company of other interested parties, at a specified date and time.

- A price guide may not be available, although there will be a 'reserve' figure set by the owner, beneath which they will not sell. The bidder offering the highest price above the reserve will be successful.

- Once a bid has been accepted, an exchange of contracts is immediate. Consequently, all legal, financial and survey enquiries will need to be completed by the buyer prior to the auction taking place. The mortgage must be in place, and a deposit available.

There are also two further matters which must be considered:

- Keep to an agreed budget and do not allow the enthusiasm and competition of other bidders to encourage you to exceed this limit.

- Money will need to be spent on surveys, solicitors etc, even if your bid is ultimately unsuccessful.

The Internet

Most estate agencies have their own websites. It is the equivalent of a virtual shop front, open 24 hours a day. For the first time buyer this is an ideal place to visit. It provides the opportunity to investigate an area without the cost and effort of travelling. It may also offer the chance to send your property requirements to the company by email. By all means use this service but also telephone and visit if possible; as I mentioned before there is no substitute for personal contact.

Unfortunately, there are shortcomings to these websites:

- If managed by a third party, property details can be out of date, and properties offered may already be sold subject to contract.

- Finding sites among the millions of pages in cyberspace can be difficult unless you know the company's web address. Use a search engine such as Google or Yahoo. Look for the website addresses in agents' local newspaper advertisements or on 'For Sale' boards. Internet portals (virtual warehouses containing information and web addresses on sites in specific subject areas) are a good source of information.

Private Sales

Buying a property directly from the owner without using estate agents is a further option.

On the plus side

- The owner may reduce the price of his property because he has saved paying commission.

- Direct contact with the owner may appeal to a purchaser who doesn't like dealing through intermediaries.

On the down side

- There is no estate agent to advise you during the sale.

- Should problems occur there is no intermediary, and you will need to confront the owner yourself.

Private sales are advertised in several ways:

- Advertisements in the classified section of local newspapers

- Advertising in local shop windows

- Creating a website with details and pictures of the property for sale

- A home made 'For Sale' board erected outside the property

- I saw a creative individual use his car as a roving advertisement by placing details of his property on a card in the back window.

Use Your Initiative – Find a House for Yourself
Some years ago, I decided to move from suburbia and relocate to the country. Unfortunately, there was very little for sale in the areas I wanted, and competition was fierce for the few houses available. With my own flat under offer, time was against me. Each week I contacted the local estate agents and scanned the newspapers, but with no success. Eventually I realised I couldn't rely on these options, and a more creative approach was needed.

I picked four roads, in an area I liked, and hand delivered

leaflets. These were very simple and created on my computer. The wording read:

> '*I apologise for contacting you in this fashion but I am keen to move into your area. Unfortunately, there is little for sale at the moment. If you had considered moving I would be very happy to hear from you.*
>
> *I should also add that I am a private individual and not an estate agent seeking business.*
>
> *I look forward to hearing from you.*'

Delivering them was an opportunity to find any 'For Sale' boards that had just appeared. It also helped increase my knowledge of the area, and discover any hidden cul-de-sac of homes I hadn't noticed before.

My next step would have been to visit local shops and public houses to 'spread the word' that I wanted to move into the village. Word of mouth can be a very powerful tool in closely-knit communities. I had also intended to place an advertisement in the local newspaper's classified section (a shorter version of the leaflet). Its aim was to unearth homes that were soon to be for sale. However, I found a property before receiving any responses.

'If you want something done then do it yourself' is the lesson learnt here.

Conclusion – The Savvy Buyer
Whether following the traditional route of visiting estate agents or taking advantage of technology and the internet, there are plenty of places to search for properties for sale. It just takes perseverance. Set aside time, once a week, to check websites and call agents. Deliver leaflets and stay aware of what is happening in your chosen area. This will put you 'head and shoulders' above most other buyers who are content to sit and wait to be contacted.

3

THE APPOINTMENT

Television programmes about selling property have become increasingly popular; people have a fascination with other people's homes. This is no surprise to estate agents; they've known for years that the public enjoys visiting properties and seeing how others live. For the first time buyer, though, it can be a daunting experience; what questions to ask the owners, what features to look for, how inquisitive can you reasonably be? This is our next topic.

Arranging the Appointment

BEING SELECTIVE
After the previous chapter, you probably have an avalanche of property details. Divide these into three groups:

Those that seem suitable.

Those that leave you undecided.

Those that fail to meet the criteria.

The list of requirements, made in the preparation stage, will be useful. The most important factors were probably:

- Price

- Location

- Room size

- Accommodation.

Followed by

- Condition and

- Special features (i.e. fireplaces, period features, garden)

and for flats

- Length of the lease

- Charges involved (e.g. service charge and ground rent).

The 'seems suitable' category is our first priority. View these immediately. Next, are there any in the 'undecided' group worthy of re-consideration? As discussed earlier, stay open-minded. As for the last category, 'unsuitable homes', keep these; they are useful as a guide to property prices in the area.

BOOKING THE APPOINTMENT

Organise only three or four in a day. Any more and eyes glaze over, concentration wanes and the process becomes tiring. To aid the memory, take notes (but ask the owner's permission).

Be selective about the viewing times. Avoid the dark. It can conceal a multitude of sins such as a shabby exterior, a poor looking roof, etc.

If the property is on a main road then visit during rush hour to check the noise level. Noise considerations at different times of day also apply to properties near schools, public houses, noisy factories or plant, dog kennels, aerodromes and places of worship. Be very careful about proximity to railway lines or busy airport flight paths. Lastly choose times when neighbours are at home, to gauge the available parking, and noise levels. This is certainly true if buying a flat in a block (although a quiet neighbour today can be replaced by a 'neighbour from hell' tomorrow).

All appointments are organised through the estate agent. Use the opportunity to ask about the circumstances surrounding the sale (which will help later when making an offer):

- Are they the only company marketing the property? If not, perhaps this suggests that the owner is keen to sell.

- How long has the property been on the market? If many months, maybe the owner will consider an offer?

- Is the property still for sale? Imagine walking around that 'perfect' home only to be told by the owner that they accepted an offer two days ago.

- Have any previous sales fallen through after survey? If so, why? Although there is no obligation on the agent to reveal this information, there is no harm in asking. If there is a 'defect', better to know now.

Other aspects of viewing:

- Security. Avoid viewing alone (or at the very least make sure someone knows where you are). Keep a mobile phone handy.

- Do not expect an estate agent to drive you to appointments; have your own transport.

- Be on time for an appointment, or ring if delayed (if this is after office hours, ask the agent for the owner's home telephone number).

- Unless time is very tight, avoid initially viewing properties 'from the outside', as it is just too difficult to judge the size and quality of a home from its exterior.

The Viewing

There are five elements to a successful viewing, and the clever buyer will exploit them all to help make a decision on the suitability of the property:

a)   superficially, does the property meet your requirements?

b)   ask the right questions of the homeowner

c)   are there indications of defects at the property?

d)   is the area suitable?

e)   never rely on a single visit.

a)   MEETING YOUR REQUIREMENTS

This needs little explanation. Your first priority is to confirm that the property's accommodation, layout and condition are satisfactory. However, as discussed before, keep these requirements flexible. This is particularly true when it comes to considering 'condition'. Always look beyond the superficiality. A dirty or poorly kept home, for example, can be transformed with only a minimum of effort. It is possible to buy a property at a reasonable price which has been dismissed by others simply because of its poor presentation. Also be mindful that a beautifully decorated home, which is probably highly priced, will quickly lose its glamour with wear and tear. It may also be concealing problems behind its alluring façade.

b)   QUESTIONS

Some years ago, I met a couple who had bought a property, and then discovered it had subsidence (a structural defect, caused by movement, which can manifest itself as cracking in the walls). They only noticed this after moving in and opening wardrobe doors in the main bedroom for the first time. The wardrobes had no backs, and cracks were visible in the wall behind. This alerted them to a problem, which ultimately proved to be serious. The property had structural defects, resolved only by relying on an insurance claim, creating a lot of stress and worry for the couple. The moral of this story is never be afraid to ask questions of the owner or seek permission to investigate something in more detail:

●   Is the garage large enough for your car?

●   What are the neighbours like?

●   Are there receipts and current guarantees for work undertaken at the property i.e. damp course, electrical wiring, extensions etc?

●   How long has the property been on the market?

- Why is the owner moving?

- When does the owner want to move?

- Are there any defects to the property or outstanding insurance claims you need to be aware of?

- Is there any unfinished work to be completed?

- What fixtures are being taken, including those in the garden, like plants or the shed?

- Are the ground rent and maintenance payments (for a flat) up to date?

- Are there any major works planned or heavy expenditure expected (at a block of flats)?

This is also a good chance to raise the subject of building construction. Properties are built in a number of ways, including steel framed, timber framed, brick and block, and concrete. For example, while many homes have external walls of brick and then a second lining of concrete block, others employ a timber frame to support the building.

Often it is difficult from appearance alone to tell which of these has been used. Information from the owner, estate agent or surveyor will be needed. It is important to obtain this, as these materials can have a direct influence on the price paid, ability to obtain a mortgage, and resaleability. Some mortgage lenders, for example, may decline to lend on a particular type of construction. Because this will leave the property with a more 'minority appeal', its asking price should be lower and reselling it later may prove difficult. Unfortunately, a book of this size cannot do this subject justice, and it is one better dealt with by further research or a conversation with a surveyor, estate agent or financial adviser.

c)   PLAYING SHERLOCK HOLMES – INDICATIONS OF
      DEFECTS
It is said that 'a little knowledge can be a dangerous thing'. This section therefore needs to be read with great caution. It is a very basic guide and certainly not exhaustive as to signs of

possible defects in a property. Keep them in mind during your visit. Ask the surveyor to investigate further should the sale be pursued.

1.   The walk to the front door offers the first indication of a property's condition.

     •   Window frames. In need of repair or replacing? Has double glazing been installed (inspect these carefully as some modern single glazed windows look 'double glazed')?

     •   Do the roof and chimney look in reasonable condition? A pair of binoculars will help identify whether any tiles are missing or have slipped. If the roof is beginning to 'show its age' then it may be necessary to renew it completely rather than just 'paper over the cracks' by repairing it. With the binoculars to hand also examine the guttering. Is it the modern plastic variety, or older metal type? Are there signs of leaking, suggesting poor condition, or a blockage from things such as leaves, that needs investigation?

     •   Are there cracks in the walls? This might be the sign of structural defects (such as subsidence) and will demand further investigation by a qualified surveyor. It can be caused by close proximity to a large tree whose roots are extracting excessive amounts of water from the ground. As the moisture content of the ground changes so this can destabilise the building or parts of it and cause 'movement'. New properties, though, may also have cracking, but probably because a newly built home takes time to 'bed down' into its surroundings. It is remedied by the builder repairing the cracks (a process called 'snagging').

     •   What is the condition of the brickwork, and the mortar binding it? Although it is only a minor item, employing a professional to 'repoint' because the mortar is disintegrating can be a costly exercise.

2.   As you walk around the building do the floors feel springy? This could be the effect of 'dry rot', a fungus that affects timbers. It can travel throughout a building and may require major remedial work to resolve. Its companion, however, 'wet rot' is less of an issue. It causes timbers to become brittle, but can be halted if the affected areas are replaced. There are numerous companies dealing with woodworm and damp matters that provide advice on this subject.

3.   Stains on walls suggest

   • Damp penetrating through from the exterior due to perhaps leaking guttering or a failing 'flat roof' (a cheaper form of roofing often found in properties that have been extended).

   • A previous (or ongoing) leak from water pipes above.

   • Condensation. Often occurs in bathrooms with poor ventilation.

   • Moisture may be penetrating the interior at ground level, as rising damp. This can be both visible or as an odour. A new damp course will remedy this (a membrane that acts as a barrier to the moisture).

4.   While walking around a room or hallway does it feel as if the floor is uneven or sloping to one side? Do the interior doors close properly and are the frames around them square? If not, then this could be a structural defect, i.e. the home is 'moving' and will definitely need further investigation. Without insulting the homeowner, politely quiz him about this. If he is aware of such structural problems, then avoid this home, even if an insurance claim is pending. It might be a situation worthy of consideration when buying your third or fourth home, but certainly not your first.

5.   How old is the central heating boiler? Does it look worn and battered? Does any of its exterior look corroded? If so, it could be coming to the end of its life. Even if all

seems well, exterior appearances can be deceptive. Ask whether the boiler is regularly serviced, and have this confirmed by your solicitor and surveyor. During the winter months, ask to see the boiler actually working, including the timer if it has one. Check also that the radiators heat up properly.

6. Has the property been altered in any way, and if so were the necessary permissions obtained (building regulations and/or planning permissions)? For example

    a) an adjoining lounge and dining room which have been combined into one through-lounge

    b) rooms that have been built into the loft

    c) extensions

    d) the removal of chimney breasts.

7. What are the water pipes made of? Lead is now frowned upon for health reasons.

8. Are there any artexed ceilings (or other roof coverings) which might contain asbestos fibres, which have health implications? The same could be true, for example, for certain garage roof coverings. These matters will need advice from a surveyor.

9. Are there streams or rivers close by that may lead to flooding?

10. What condition are the boundary fences in? If in need of repair who is responsible for them?

11. While not a 'defect', ask whether anyone has rights over the property i.e. restrictive covenants and easements. These are legal matters but ones that a buyer should be aware of. The first is a restriction placed on the property to stop something being done with it. For example a restrictive covenant might be that the building cannot be used as a place of work, or cannot be altered in some way. The

second type, the easement, is a right that someone has over your land. Some years ago I was considering buying a cottage until I noticed gates at the end of the garden. These were to allow the neighbours to enter my garden, trundling their wheelie bins behind them, to reach an access road at the end of the row of houses, from where the bin men collected the refuse each week. This is called a 'right of way' and may affect the price of the property (and certainly affected my decision to buy it!).

12. Again, not a defect but ask whether there are any shared drains on the property and who is responsible for their upkeep.

d) BEYOND THE FRONT DOOR

Buying a home involves not only its suitability, but also that of the area around it. Investigate the surrounding roads, and be mindful of

- Noisy children in the road that might disturb you if you are a shift worker

- Burnt out cars or boarded shop fronts that suggest a problem area

- Parking restrictions

- How well are the communal areas of a block of flats maintained?

Reading local newspapers can also provide clues to an area, and help us make a more informed decision about buying our first home.

e) REFRESHING THE MEMORY – NEVER RELY ON A SINGLE VISIT

Before making a decision about the property, arrange a second visit (unless there are already other interested parties, and time is against you). There are certain to be features you failed to notice the first time e.g.:

- Is that second bedroom really large enough?

- Didn't the kitchen seem bigger the first time?

- 'There are more steps to this second floor flat than I remember.'

- 'I never realised how close the maisonette was to the school playground.'

- Does the flat have loft space?

Use this opportunity for all parties involved with the purchase, or who have a financial interest, to see the property. If, for example, a couple are buying their first home, then both need to see it. This is too important a matter for decisions to made on someone else's behalf. Another example is of the first time buyer relying on parents for his deposit. Mum and dad are likely to want to be part of the decision making process, so confirm their agreement during this second visit. Before a final decision is made, an internal inspection by all parties involved is a necessity.

4

THE OFFER

Having decided on the right property, the next step is to make an offer. The main difficulty at this stage is deciding on an offer price which is both affordable for the buyer and an acceptable figure for the seller. Feelings of tension surface, excitement levels rise, there is a tangible sense of anticipation in the air ... and this is just the reaction of the estate agent!

The offer process is divided into four sections:

- Preparation

- The offer

- Negotiation

- Acceptance

Preparation

The law in this country is far from perfect when it comes to buying a residential property. A buyer or seller can withdraw at any time and for any reason prior to 'exchange of contracts'. This is a devastating experience, and is often due to lack of preparation. Problems occur that should have been addressed at the start, if the relevant groundwork had been done. The following questions will help.

ASK YOURSELF:

- Do we need to see the property again before making an offer?

Would it help to arrange a further visit with someone who can provide an unbiased opinion?

If there are future plans to alter the property structurally, take a builder with you for advice (having asked the owner's permission).

- Has the area around the property been investigated thoroughly?

Travel to the property using different routes, and at different times of the day and week, to highlight any features that may not have been obvious before.

- Speak to the police about the level of crime in the area and 'neighbourhood watch' schemes. Read the local papers for a few weeks if you live some distance away, to get an idea of the local 'culture'.

- Ask the local council for information. Is this a conservation area and subject to building restrictions? Are there proposed developments nearby or changes in transport/ shopping facilities that may affect the price in the future? (Although a solicitor will investigate these matters later, better to ask now before making an offer.) If the reason for buying the property is to take advantage of a school's catchment area, is this guaranteed by moving to the property?

ASK THE OWNER:

- The offer figure.

Ask the owner for guidance on an acceptable offer – this will give you an idea of whether the offer you have in mind is a realistic one.

- What does the asking price include?

Carpets and curtains normally remain but, if not, then budget for them in the offer.

- Does he know the history of the property?

Is it a purpose built three-bedroom house or actually a two-bedroom property which has been extended? If so, ensure that the legal documents, such as the Planning Permission and Building Control (Regulations) Approval, are available for this building work.

- Will the vendor sell, regardless of finding another property to buy?

Will he move into rented accommodation, or do you need to wait for him to find a property to buy? How long will this take?

- Has the vendor already found a property to buy? If so, is there a 'chain' and how many others are involved? A 'chain' means that the first time buyer is reliant not only on his own purchase, but several others. It would take only one of these to fail, and the chain collapses like a pack of cards. Once you have discovered whether there is a chain, and how long it is, you can assess the level of risk involved and make an informed decision about whether to progress.

ASK THE ESTATE AGENT:

- How long has the property been on the market? If it's longer than a couple of months, the owner may well consider an offer (especially if he has already found another home to buy).

- Is there more than one estate agent marketing the property? If so, this could suggest that the owner is keen to sell and may accept an offer.

- Is there anything detrimental to the property that you need to be made aware of? For example

  1. Does anyone else have rights over your land (called easements and covenants)?

  2. Has planning permission (e.g. for an extension) ever been refused?

3. Has anyone previously withdrawn from buying the property and why? If a sale has failed due to a poor survey, then why waste your own time and money?

4. Have there been insurance claims for subsidence?

5. What utilities does the property offer? Some blocks of flats have no gas supply and rely wholly on electricity.

6. When buying a home on a newly built estate, will any of the other houses be sold to housing associations? This could diminish the saleability of the property in the future.

7. With a flat, what type of residents live in the block? While this can change continually, are some of the flats council owned, or managed by a housing association? Will this devalue your home?

OTHER CONSIDERATIONS

As discussed on page 24, stamp duty can add considerably to the cost of buying a home. Properties above £60,000 but below £250,000 are currently liable for a 1% government tax on the whole amount, while this increases to 3% for those between £250,001 to £500,000.

Take the example of a property priced at £260,000. An offer of £255,000 would incur 3% stamp duty at £7,650 (3% x £255,000). However, agree a sale at £249,000 and the stamp duty is decreased to 1% i.e. £2,490 (1% x £249,000) (please note that these percentages are used as an example; rates and thresholds are subject to change).

In this particular situation, if the owner is adamant that only £252,000 would be acceptable, then perhaps a figure of £250,000 could be agreed. The extra £2,000 would account for 'fixtures and fittings' i.e. carpets, curtains. Fixtures and fittings are not subject to stamp duty, therefore this would reduce the 3% stamp duty to 1%. However, this is only possible if this amount is deemed to be reasonable by the Inland Revenue. To confirm this, a form now needs to be completed by the buyer regarding stamp duty (in force since December 2003). The Land Transaction Return ensures that unacceptable amounts are not being allocated to 'fixtures and fittings' in order to deprive the state of its revenue.

Once completed, the form is then scrutinised by the Inland Revenue to confirm that the correct amount of stamp duty has been paid, and not avoided by overstating the value of fixtures and fittings in order to bring the sale price into a lower stamp duty bracket. It is a lengthy eight pages, and will probably be completed by the buyer's solicitor (if asked nicely!) and then signed by the buyer. Information required will include details regarding the property, stamp duty amount and purchaser.

If in any doubt about how much can be allocated to fixtures and fittings, consult your solicitor.

The Offer
The estate agent will need approximately 10–15 minutes with you to go through the 'offer taking' process. His task is to

• Present the owner with the maximum amount of relevant information about a potential purchaser, and

• Ensure all circumstances surrounding this potential buyer's offer are known, in order to diminish the risk of any problems occurring later in the sale.

QUESTIONS ASKED
These will include:

Contact Details
Provide as much information as possible, in case you're needed urgently during the sale.

Has everyone involved in the sale seen the property?
Is there anyone else who needs to view the property before the offer can be made?

When do you want to move?
Do your timescales match those of the owners? For example:

• If you live in rented accommodation and need to give a period of notice (although it is too early to alert your landlord)

• If holidays are planned.

Do you have a connection with anyone at the estate agents?
In order to comply with the 1979 Estate Agents Act the agent
will need to know if you are a relative, or connected with any
member of staff at the agency.

The Amount
Come prepared with a figure (plucking one out of thin air will
not instil confidence in the agent or owner!). Deciding on a
figure is a balancing act between wanting to buy for the cheapest
price, and not wanting to insult the owner with an embarrass-
ingly low figure. Being aware of prices in the area will help, as
will some of the questions discussed previously:

●   Are other parties interested in the property?

Although the estate agent is working on behalf of his client (the
homeowner) and may be tempted to suggest that a property has
proved more popular than it actually has, the Estate Agents Act
states that it is unlawful for the agent to suggest that there are
other offers when this is untrue. However, if a property is being
marketed by multiple agents, your agent may be unaware of
offers being submitted through other companies.

●   Has the property been on the market for some time?

●   Have the owners found another home to buy?

Whatever the offer, leave yourself room to negotiate further.
    If the property market is falling then this is reason enough to
ensure that the price paid is as realistic as possible. However, there
are circumstances when it is wise to offer as much as possible
immediately:

●   When other parties are interested

●   When the property market is rising quickly. Losing this
      home might mean having to pay a higher price for a
      similar one in the near future.

The goal is to make an offer attractive enough to persuade the
owner to accept immediately, and refuse to deal with any other
buyers. To reduce the possibility of heartache later, ask that the

property be removed from the market if a sale is agreed. If refused, suggest marketing ceases for four weeks (allowing enough time for you to prove your sincerity), and persuade the vendor to stop marketing once this 'trial' period is over. If this too is unacceptable to the owner, are you prepared to continue with the purchase knowing that the property is still on the market?

The Financial Details

The agent will need information regarding your mortgage requirements or financial arrangements. The more details you supply, the more appealing your offer will be.

Having made an offer, the agent is obliged to inform the owner in writing (and probably verbally, to speed up the process). It is an unwritten rule that offers are made on properties one at a time. On the few occasions I dealt with buyers who offered on several properties simultaneously, it suggested that they were not committed to any of them and had little consideration for anyone but themselves. Not an image that will endear you to homeowners or estate agents.

Negotiation

As a first time buyer you are in a strong position; no chain and able to offer an immediate sale. If, however, this is not enough to persuade a homeowner to accept your first offer, then ask the estate agent what figure the vendor is expecting. If the agent is not willing to commit himself, then either

- Offer the best figure you can afford, or

- Offer a little more and gauge the reaction (remembering 'Jager's Law'; the longer the negotiation the less chance of success).

If negotiations become protracted, but the desire to purchase is still strong then

- Suggest a final figure, asking that certain 'fixtures and fittings' be included e.g. curtains, free standing wardrobes etc, or

- Look at the possibility of increasing the mortgage or deposit to bridge the gap. Think carefully, and beware of being swept along in the excitement of the moment. Buying a property means making regular monthly mortgage payments and not becoming overstretched financially. If necessary, arrange another appointment to confirm that this property really does warrant another offer.

If having followed these suggestions an agreement is still no closer, consider withdrawing. Life is too short to endure the stress brought on by long negotiations. Your time and energy could be better spent finding another home.

GAZUMPING

One of the major flaws in the English and Welsh property system is the ability to 'gazump'. Common in a rising market, gazumping occurs when a sale is agreed, but another person then offers a higher figure, which is accepted instead. The original buyer not only loses the property, but also any money already spent on the transaction (e.g. solicitors, surveyors etc).

No one has yet devised a foolproof way to eradicate this. Asking for the property to be withdrawn from the market, once a sale has been agreed, can help (but still doesn't eliminate the possibility of a person who viewed the property weeks ago suddenly re-appearing and wanting to purchase it). A buyer can only hope that the homeowner has sincere intentions to sell to him and is strong willed enough to reject any other bids should they unexpectedly materialise. This attitude is more likely if the buyer shows willing from the start of the sale, by

- Setting the finances and legal matters in motion immediately

- Offering close enough to the asking price to leave other interested buyers little opportunity to beat his offer.

Acceptance

If the offer is accepted, it's time for a small celebration – you are a major step closer to buying your first home. But before breaking open that bottle of 'bubbly' there is a little 'housekeeping' to take care of ...

- Confirm that the property is being taken off the market, if this has been agreed. The cynical among you might even ask friends to ring the agent after a few days, mention that they saw that property for sale, and ask if they can view it!

- Show willing by immediately providing your solicitor's details to the estate agent.

- Remain philosophical – a sale agreed is only half the battle.

Footnote. An offer is given 'subject to contract'. This is an important phrase, and should be added to any offer you submit in writing. It is your 'get out' clause, and allows you to withdraw at any time up to exchange of contracts.

5

AFTER THE SALE IS AGREED

The Next Steps
Having agreed the sale, the next step is dependent upon the owner's situation. If he still needs to find a property to buy, it is sensible to wait before proceeding further. Avoid spending money until the chain is complete. If the chain *is* complete, or the owner is prepared to move out anyway, then complete the mortgage forms and instruct the solicitor. The estate agent will send a 'Memorandum of Sale'. This letter confirms the sale and includes:

- The price agreed

- Details of the purchaser, owner, and their solicitors

- Conditions relating to the sale, e.g. timescales

- Items to remain at the property (fixtures and fittings).

Although this is not a legally binding document, it is important to check that the information is correct and includes the phrase 'subject to contract' (see footnote on previous page).

THE SOLICITOR
It is now time to put your solicitor to work, and ask him to begin the legal process. You may be asked to pay for immediate expenses, and to sign a copy of the solicitor's 'Business Terms and Conditions'. Proof of identity and address will also be required, e.g. passport, driving licence etc, to comply with money laundering regulations.

The solicitor will confirm that:

- You understand the commitment you are about to make

- You have organised a mortgage lender and a deposit

- You are aware of the finances needed to maintain a home.

The owner's solicitor will then send legal paperwork to your solicitor, although these procedures, including searches, are increasingly being done electronically. The material will include:

- *A contract.* This document, called an 'Agreement Including Standard Conditions Of Sale' contains both general matters relating to all sales, and those specific to yours. Two copies of the contract are sent to your solicitor for his approval. One will be retained, and the other sent back to the seller's solicitor once the details are approved (this will eventually be signed by the seller prior to the 'exchange of contracts').

- *'Seller's Property Information Form'.* This is completed by the homeowner and his solicitor, and covers a wide range of subjects: the property's boundaries, guarantees for work undertaken at the property (double glazing, electrical work etc), disputes with neighbours, any alterations to the property and necessary permissions, and the proposed moving date. If a leasehold property is being sold then an additional form, the *'Seller's Leasehold Information Form'*, will also be supplied. This confirms the length of lease, service and ground rent charges, and names those responsible for the upkeep of the building.

- Fixtures and fittings list.

Based on the answers in the Seller's Information Form, the buyer's solicitor may raise further questions, called 'additional enquiries'.

THE SEARCHES
Searches are documents dealing with the property that is being bought, and the area surrounding it. Organised by the purchaser's solicitor, there are several types of search, including:

- *Local Authority Search:* This is in two parts:

  a)   the LLC1 form which details charges on the property such as conditional planning consents, improvement grants, tree preservation orders and conservation areas

  b)   the Con 29 form which covers matters under the council's jurisdiction e.g. proposed housing or commercial developments nearby, proposed new roads etc.

- *Drainage Search:* concerned with drainage and sewage in the area.

- *Environmental Search:* depending on circumstances, this may be necessary if, for example, the property has been built on a landfill site or in an area of flooding. It covers a 500m radius of the building.

- *Coal Search:* this deals with information about any local mines, e.g. housing built in the neighbourhood of old mine shafts in areas such as Lancashire, Yorkshire, Derbyshire, Kent, or Warwickshire.

Mortgage and Survey
The relevant mortgage forms need to be completed and a survey fee paid. The latter is one of the most important stages of the buying process, and needs further explanation.

Buying a first home is a major commitment. To be certain that a property is good security for the loan to be made against it, and fair value, you and/or the mortgage lender will employ a qualified surveyor to investigate matters pertaining to its construction, value and condition, and detail these in a report.

There are three types of surveys available:

- Mortgage lender's valuation.

- Home buyer's survey and valuation (also called homebuyer's report or homebuyer's service).

- Building survey (also known as a structural survey).

Mortgage lender's valuation: this is the most basic of the three and mainly for the benefit of the lender. It confirms that the property is worthy of a mortgage. This is the least expensive type, sometimes free, and should not be relied upon to answer the questions necessary to make an informed decision about a purchase (its contents may not even be made available to the buyer).

Home buyer's survey and valuation: although more costly than the first, it is a far more detailed document. Written in a clear and understandable way, it is a standard form with the purpose of a) offering an opinion on the sale price and b) highlighting significant problems or defects that need immediate attention. If appropriate, any associated legal and environmental matters will also be mentioned. The 'home buyer's survey and valuation' is used for homes in average condition and of standard construction. Those buying a property which has been greatly altered, is in poor condition or of unusual construction should consider our final survey type.

The building survey: this looks in depth at the property, and leaves 'few stones unturned'! Because it is concerned with condition, construction and defects both large and small, it is a lengthy document and consequently the most expensive. While the mortgage lender can arrange the first two types of survey, a buyer would need to commission this one himself.

A question often asked by people purchasing a newly built home is whether a survey is really necessary. Apart from it being a prerequisite by the mortgage lender, it would be unwise to enter into a transaction without one, even for a very recently constructed home. While there should be a building guarantee called a 'NHBC Guarantee', it is better to be armed with as much information as possible before the purchase than regret it later should a problem appear. Only a survey can fulfil this.

Reading The Survey

Once completed, the survey is normally sent to the purchaser with the mortgage offer. For a first time buyer, this might be his first experience of seeing a survey report. For those receiving the popular 'home buyer's survey and valuation', I have always thought it is very much like reading a national newspaper – you turn to the back page for the sports and then wade through the less important matters, like the economy and world politics! The final page is one of the most interesting. It is the summary, and includes the surveyor's overall opinion of the property, its worth and any issues that need to be addressed.

As the complete report can be many pages long, it demands to be read slowly and several times. Use a marker to highlight passages or technical words not understood, and make notes in the margins as questions come to mind. The surveyor can then be called to answer these. If you have a good relationship with your solicitor, call on his expertise to offer a second opinion. The estate agent can be asked but remember that he represents the owner and may not have in-depth knowledge of building construction.

THE PROBLEM CLINIC

We have all heard terrible tales about problems which occur while buying a home. The majority of issues, however, are resolvable (otherwise, all estate agents would be poor!). While mentioning every problem that *could* occur would take a whole book of its own, here are some of the most common.

1.   A POOR SURVEY

It is unlikely that the survey will be perfect. Properties are constructed with materials that, like everything else, are affected by normal wear and tear. The survey report may, therefore, unearth matters that need closer inspection.

- *Damp*: moisture has penetrated the interior of a building. Unless extensive, it can be remedied for relatively little cost (although redecoration may be involved).

- *Woodworm:* like damp, this is quite common and usually rectifiable, depending on how far it has spread.

- *Leaking roof*

- *Leaking guttering*

- *Electrical wiring*: wiring that fails to conform to the most modern standards is not unusual. Ask the surveyor how much of an immediate or real problem this is.

Many purchasers, faced with any of these, panic and ask either for an immediate reduction on the price, or withdraw from the sale altogether. How can such decisions be made, though, without being in possession of all the facts? Instead, it is better to discover whether the problem is as severe as it seems, and how much it will cost to rectify. Bearing in mind the amount of time and effort already invested in the sale, what harm could there be in waiting a few more days for this information?

Arrange for specialists to visit the property and inspect the defects i.e. a 'damp and woodworm' company, a roofer, etc. Organise two of each to call and offer an opinion and a price (there may be costs involved, so check).

Armed with their quotes, it is time to make a decision about the purchase. If the costs are small, you might decide to ignore the problem and continue with the sale. If not, then the vendor is approached, via the estate agent, and a price reduction asked for, to take into account the extra money that now needs to be spent. To prove the request is legitimate, provide a copy of the survey and contractor's estimates. The estate agent will then report to the vendor and return with one of three answers:

- The reduction is acceptable. The price is altered and the sale continues (the solicitors and financial adviser need to be informed. A price reduction may affect the percentage of mortgage being obtained, which could have other 'knock on' effects. A financial adviser will be able to provide advice on this).

- The owner refuses any reduction. The purchaser must now decide whether he wishes to continue at the original price (taking into account the money already spent, and the prospect of having to pay more for the next property if the market is rising).

- The owner wants to negotiate. Using the estate agent as an intermediary, you will try to find 'common ground' that keeps all parties happy.

2. UNDERTAKING REPAIRS

If the survey highlights necessary repairs, never ask the owner to undertake them. Instead, agree a reduction and arrange the work yourself. Better to deal with tradesmen of your choosing and quality.

It is unlikely that the owner will allow this work to be undertaken immediately, preferring instead that you wait until after 'completion', when you have legal ownership of the property. The only exception might be when dealing with a property which is vacant and in need of renovation. The purchaser can then request access to the property after exchange and before completion to make the home habitable. The owner is under no obligation to agree, but consent is often considered if the purchaser signs a document called an 'undertaking', which outlines the jobs being undertaken and confirms that the buyer will:

- Be liable for any damage caused

- Agree not to take up residency until completion.

This can be organised through the solicitors, and is best agreed upon before exchange of contracts.

3. WITHDRAWING FROM A SALE

Occasionally, there may be the need to withdraw from a sale. This could be due to the buyer's situation altering suddenly, such as change of job or financial circumstances, or as the result of a poor survey. If so, inform your solicitor and the homeowner. This may be unpleasant, but it is courteous. I have dealt with buyers who have decided against buying a property and failed to inform anyone for weeks! This is selfish and unnecessary.

4. THE OWNER'S SLOW SOLICITOR

If the legal paperwork is slow coming from the owner's solicitor, then the buyer's solicitor needs to question why.

- Is the vendor's solicitor simply over burdened with work?

- Has the vendor's solicitor been told to slow the process down? Is the vendor negotiating with another buyer? Does he have a hidden agenda that the buyer is unaware of? Is he having second thoughts about moving? Does the vendor have a problem with the property he is hoping to buy? These questions can be asked by both the buyer's solicitor and by the estate agent. The latter will be keen to help as he is only paid when the sale is completed.

- Is the vendor's solicitor in possession of all the necessary documents? If not, when will these be ready?

5. MORTGAGE CONDITIONS

When the mortgage offer is issued, the purchaser needs to read it through carefully. Confirm that it contains the correct interest rate and amount to be borrowed. There will also be a section which outlines any conditions attached to the mortgage that need to be fulfilled. These might include further documents required by the mortgage lender, or additional reports on the building (such as an electrical inspection or damp report).

6. DEFECTIVE LEASE

One of the most important elements when buying a flat or maisonette is ensuring that the lease is satisfactory, as it defines the responsibilities and obligations of those who own properties in the building with regards to the freeholder and each owner of the flats.

As standards have changed over the years, your solicitor may feel that the lease is inadequate or has errors. Such defects might include insufficient details about assigning responsibilities for the foundation, roof and communal areas like hallways and landings. While this may come as a disappointment, it is a matter that can be rectified. A 'deed of variation' is required. As the name suggests, this is a legal term for a process which involves changing aspects of the lease to bring it in line with more modern procedures. It can take time to organise, and your solicitor will be able to advise as to whether it is worth pursuing.

7. LEASE EXTENSION

Another important aspect when buying a flat is the length of the lease. One in excess of 75–80 years is preferable. However, it may be possible to make an offer on a property with a shorter lease, but then extend it before the end of the transaction (completion). There will be costs involved:

- The cost of extending the lease

- Solicitors' fees

- Additional costs to other related parties, which includes paying the freeholder's costs e.g. his managing agent who has supervision of the building on behalf of the freeholder, his solicitor, and his surveyor who 'values' the cost of extending the lease.

If the vendor is keen to sell and the short lease is proving a problem then he may bear the majority, if not all, of the costs and would be expected to extend the lease before completion. (The buyer should also be aware that one disadvantage of extending a lease is that it may mean the ground rent increases.)

8.   INCORRECT DETAILS

If, as the sale progresses, it transpires that the property sheet given to the buyer by the estate agent was incorrect, action can be taken. Under the 1991 Property Misdescriptions Act (PMA) all property details supplied by an estate agent must be accurate. If not, then they breach the PMA. For example:

- The property details show that a flat has 97 years of lease but subsequent documentation shows it to be only 79 years

- A garden described by the estate agent as 100ft is actually 75ft

- A property described by the estate agent as being in good order actually requires modernisation

- A home marketed as a 'new instruction' has been on the market for many months.

Such matters have gone unchecked in the past, but the PMA has put paid to these 'errors'. If this situation arises, then either:

- Approach the owner of the estate agency and explain the situation. He will want to rectify matters immediately and may offer to pay some compensation if inconvenience has been caused, for example if a party has travelled some distance to view a property based on misleading information.

If this does not bring satisfactory results then the next option is to

- Call the local Trading Standards Office. They will investigate the matter and decide whether further action is needed. It is important to note that their assistance can be requested, even if you are not actually buying a property but simply in possession of property details that have been misleading. If necessary, they have the power to seize items from a company to prove a breach of the Property Misdescriptions Act. The act is enforced through the courts and if found guilty the company and individual involved can be subject to penalties such as a fine and even a criminal record.

9. BE PRO-ACTIVE

Although we employ 'professionals' to deal with property sales, don't sit back and rely on them wholly. Keep in contact regularly and ask questions to confirm that everything is proceeding to plan. For example:

The Mortgage Broker

- Has the survey been organised. If not, why not?

- Have all the necessary employer's references and credit checks been sent to the mortgage lender?

- With the survey completed, when will the mortgage offer appear?

- If the mortgage offer is delayed, ask for specific reasons why.

The Solicitor

- Have the necessary documents been received from the owner's solicitor?

- If buying a flat, have all the documents relating to the lease and maintenance charges been received?

- If legal paperwork is outstanding, when is this to be chased and by whom?

The Estate Agent
The agent has the best overall view of the sale and any associated chain. He is ideally placed to chase:

- Outstanding paperwork

- Delayed surveys

and keep abreast of progress in the chain.

Never be afraid to ring and ask your estate agent for advice; it is in his financial interest for the sale to be successful. There is little an estate agent cannot do if he is experienced and skilful.

Preparing for Exchange
With any problems resolved, the next step is exchange of contracts. This is the point of no return, at which the vendor becomes legally bound to sell, and the purchaser legally bound to buy.

THE SOLICITOR
Before exchange of contracts, the solicitor will need to be in possession of all of the necessary legal documents, comprising:

- Contract

- Searches

- Enquiries

- Satisfactory mortgage offer

- Leasehold documents if a flat is being bought

- Transfer documents

- Deposit.

The purchaser will then visit the solicitor's office (or use the post/email/fax etc) to discuss these matters and take any final advice. Confirm that the sale includes all that was expected, in particular:

- The 'fixtures and fittings' list is in order

- The completion date is correct (when deciding on this, take into account the availability of removal vans)

- If it was requested that areas be cleared of all rubbish (i.e. garage or loft) has this been included in the contract?

- Are *all* the keys to be made available on completion? Few things could be more annoying than to find that keys to the garage or kitchen window have gone missing.

The contract is then signed.

DEPOSIT AND ADDITIONAL COSTS

The solicitor will require a deposit. This is normally 5%-10% of the purchase price, and non-returnable after exchange. A banker's draft or building society cheque is preferable. If notice needs to be given to obtain the deposit, then the purchaser should organise this in plenty of time. Because of growing fears about money laundering (money obtained from the proceeds of crime and transformed into legitimate funds), cash will not be acceptable.

The buyer will also need to arrange building insurance so that it can be initiated immediately after exchange. Lastly, and I only mention it again because of the large sums involved, remember that 'stamp duty' is payable by the purchaser (the solicitor usually requests payment of stamp duty after exchange and prior to completion).

THE 'EXCHANGE'

With everything organised, and the chain ready, 'exchange of contracts' can take place. This is carried out over the telephone between the solicitors in the chain. The purchaser need not be present.

It is far from an exciting event and consists of the purchaser's solicitor saying, for example, to the owner's solicitor,

'I release the contract to you under Law Society Formula B'[1]

The contract is now released, which means the purchaser's solicitor promises that for a fixed period of time he will not withdraw from the transaction. With this guarantee, the vendor's solicitor can now follow the same process on the property his client is buying. This conversation therefore is duplicated by each solicitor up the chain until it reaches the top, and all contracts are released. Calls to confirm the exchange happen next, but this time down the chain until it reaches the solicitor at the bottom. At that point all the exchanges of contracts have been confirmed.

With exchange of contracts, the finishing line is in sight; the day when you take ownership of your new home, known as Completion.

Because the period leading up to this involves so many elements common to both buyer and seller, this final part of our journey is dealt with jointly, in Part III, starting on page 115.

---

[1] There are in fact three legal mechanisms for exchanging contracts, formulas A, B and C.

PART II

FIRST TIME SELLER

6

PREPARATION

First Time Seller, First Time Buyer

Part II of the book is mainly aimed at those who were first time buyers a few years ago, and now want to sell that first house or flat and move on (to probably a larger one). But this part of the book will also be *extremely useful* to the first time buyer. The advice given here will enable a buyer to appreciate the seller's point of view; by seeing the whole procedure from the opposite perspective, a much better and more balanced picture emerges.

The purchase and sale of property is one of the very few areas of British life that involves financial negotiation, so it is an experience that is largely foreign to most of us, and that is why it is so useful to understand both sides.

Introduction

Many years ago, while studying for my degree, I attended a classical music concert. I didn't particularly want to go, but felt obliged, as many of the performers in the orchestra were friends. It didn't help that I knew they were poorly prepared for the concert.

The highlight of the evening was the performance of a beautiful symphony by Cesar Franck. As the conductor raised his baton and the orchestra started to play, one of my course tutors, who was sitting in the audience, remarked rather loudly,

"What's the point in playing the rest of the piece if they can't even get the first note in tune?"

I have never forgotten this. It serves as a good reminder that thorough preparation is *vital* before we begin any task. Those who've read the First Time Buyer section of this book will already be acquainted with this idea, and it is just as true for the first time seller. Careful planning will save time in the end, and help avoid many of the pitfalls to which others have fallen prey.

This chapter is divided into four sections:

- Preparing our home

- Preparing the paperwork

- Preparing our finances

- Preparing ourselves

Preparing Our Home
Preparing a property for sale has become a popular subject in the media. This is hardly surprising. It is as crucial to finding a buyer as are location and accommodation. I learnt early in my career that the longer an applicant spends at a property, the more likely he is to buy it. This is a good principle to remember.

If the environment is welcoming, then people are likely to stay longer and feel a greater bond with the property. This is achieved by appealing to three of our five senses; sight, sound, and smell. With these we form opinions about the world around us. Unfortunately, this can be an immediate, and sometimes unfair reaction. If a prospective buyer walks up the path to your home and is greeted with a shabby front door, he'll have a poor opinion of the property before he even sets foot in the hallway. The fact that you may have a splendid modern kitchen or beautiful marble tiled bathroom is immaterial; his mind is made up and will be difficult to change. Subconsciously he starts wondering what other problems may be lurking that are not so obvious?

This issue can be a particular challenge when selling a flat, where you are reliant on others keeping the communal parts of the block looking spotless. When I sold my flat many years ago, I took 10 minutes before a viewing to pick up any litter in the communal areas and spray air freshener around the entrance.

A PERFECT WORLD
Why are first impressions so important? Because the public often cannot be bothered to see beyond the blemishes. If a place is scruffy and there are five other homes to see that day, why

waste time with this one? To do our home justice, we need to be honest and objective.

- Could the paintwork in the lounge do with a little freshening up?

- Would the bathroom be better without the patches of condensation on the ceiling?

- And, for those of you who are keen on DIY, don't you think it's time to complete those wardrobes in the bedroom that you started building last summer?

It is difficult to be self critical because all of us become accustomed to our homes. I have met many homeowners who didn't appreciate that leaving piles of food crumbs all over the kitchen, or the dog's food partly in its bowl, but mostly on the kitchen floor, is a 'turn off' to buyers. Untidiness is another aspect. Imagine walking into a room littered with books and children's toys. How can a buyer appreciate its size or potential?

If we do not remedy these matters then we are doing our home a disservice. As sellers, we must consider how others will view it. If keeping a family house constantly tidy is a strain, then perhaps

- Limit the children/pets to one room, just prior to a viewing

- Arrange appointments for specific times, during which the property can be kept in an orderly fashion.

However you remedy the situation it will pay dividends. The more the public like our home, the more they are likely to pay for it.

FURTHER IMPROVEMENTS
Cosmetic improvements are only one area that can visually enhance a property. Light, for example, plays an important role; opening curtains during the day gives the impression of an airy room. Alternatively, if it's dark or cloudy outside, switch the lights on (if it's cold as well, then turn the thermostat up).

To appeal to our sense of sound, keep windows shut if you live on a busy main road, or play soothing classical music. This is infinitely more inviting than leaving the television on.

As regards smell, pleasing fragrances are a great help in producing a positive experience for our viewer. Baking bread has always been a popular example, and there are many supermarket fragrances that mask the everyday smells of cigarettes and cooking. Included in this category are pets. It is easy to become accustomed to their odour and be oblivious to it permeating carpets and furnishings. If anything is guaranteed to cause a potential purchaser to flee, with no intention of ever returning, it is the overpowering smell of animals. The remedy is simple; clean the garden before an appointment and mask the smell of pets. Remember that some people are allergic to or frightened of pets, so it might even be preferable to keep animals shut away during a viewing.

These improvements cost little. Avoid major expenditure. Spend your money on your new home rather than on your present one. The only exception would be obvious defects that may be mentioned on a buyer's survey such as broken guttering or a leaking roof. As a rule of thumb, if a problem can be resolved for a few hundred pounds then consider sorting it. Otherwise, expect to be asked for a discount at the offer stage or after a survey.

Preparing the Paperwork

Organising the paperwork is often overlooked, and is particularly important for properties which have undergone structural alteration. Some of the most depressing times I had as an estate agent involved selling a house with incomplete documentation. I'd find a buyer for it, and all would go well until it transpired that the owner didn't have all the legal documents needed for the extended kitchen, or the bedroom in the loft. Either the sale then fell apart, or it became a long drawn out affair as the owner tried to obtain the relevant documents. With a little forward planning this could have been organised before marketing.

Keeping receipts for major jobs such as reproofing or rewiring is also vital. Anyone can claim to have had new plumbing installed two years ago. Reinforce this with paperwork and yours will be 'head and shoulders' above the average home for sale. Flat owners will need a copy of their lease, and receipts confirming the payment of the service charge or ground rent. These are obtained from the party who receives these monies i.e. the freeholder, managing agent or residents' association. Many an undecided purchaser has been persuaded to buy a particular property because of such diligence. Until recently, title deeds were also required as proof of ownership. While for many this is still a valid system, title deeds are now redundant for property transactions completed after 13 October 2003. They instead have a document issued by the Land Registry called a Title Information Document. Plainly both systems will be in use for a number of years, and if in doubt about the whereabouts of any of these items consult your solicitor. In fact, this is the ideal time for those without a solicitor to shop around and make a choice. He can help prepare the paperwork in anticipation of securing a buyer. This is a subject that was covered in more detail on page 53.

In an effort to simplify the housing market and remove much of the stress involved with the buying process in England and Wales, a radical change to the way in which property is sold has been proposed by the government. Provisionally suggested for introduction in 2005/06, the Housing Bill, if fully enacted, will see sellers legally obliged to provide information about the property for sale to the buyer. This information will come in the form of HIPs (Home Information Packs), and will include a home condition report (survey) and all of the relevant legal details (proof of ownership, planning consents, guarantees and local authority matters). The survey will not offer any indication on value, so a traditional valuation report will also be necessary, as now expected by mortgage lenders.

It is hoped that, armed with this information, buyers will be able to make a more informed decision about the purchase earlier on in the process. In turn, this should reduce the number of sales that collapse, as well as quickening the buying process. However, there remain many matters to be clarified so it is not yet clear when exactly HIPs will come into force, if ever, or the exact procedures involved.

Preparing Our Finances
Two questions regarding our finances need to be asked:

- If we intend to buy another property when ours is sold, can we obtain the necessary loan?

- Will redeeming the present mortgage incur any penalties with our mortgage lender?

Some years ago I dealt with a young couple who found a buyer for their home, only to discover later that redeeming their mortgage early would incur a huge penalty. This was so unexpected it almost derailed the sale. Fortunately the situation was rectified but not before many sleepless nights were had by all.

Preparing Ourselves
With the paperwork, finances and property organised, just one more item remains ... preparing ourselves.

'Never let selling your home rule your life.'

I have met too many people, particularly first time sellers, who allow their sale to dominate them completely. Every waking hour is spent thinking about it. Quickly, all sense of perspective is lost; a small problem, that could be easily resolved, becomes overwhelming. It is impossible to see 'light at the end of the tunnel', and everything becomes an effort. Stress is setting in.

Selling a property is only a very small part of our lives, and should be treated as such. It is important, but not to the detriment of our well being. For example, if you eat at 7pm then leave this hour free rather than rushing the meal because you have a 7.30 viewing. If children are in bed by 8pm then finish viewings by 7.45. The public will understand.

However, you may need to be flexible if a viewer is coming a long distance to see your property and only has limited time available. You don't want to lose a possible sale because you refused to alter your usual routine!

7

CHOOSING AN ESTATE AGENT

Mr and Mrs Average want to buy a car. They visit the showroom and immediately see a vehicle they like. The salesman approaches and starts his sales pitch, explaining how wonderful the car is, its sleek lines, ample boot, fast acceleration and spacious interior. Our couple have certain requirements but instead of asking any questions, they base their decision solely on the salesman's information.

Only once the car is delivered do they realise it is a little smaller than they had wanted, the fuel consumption is not as economical as first thought, and the warranty is only for one year not the two they had expected. Quickly they regret their decision.

Obviously, this situation is ridiculous. Who would buy a car on this basis? It is instead a painstaking process, involving preparation, research, and comparison of a number of vehicles. So, when selling our most expensive asset, our home, why does this common sense approach disappear? Many homeowners give as little thought to choosing an estate agent as Mr and Mrs Average did to choosing a car. No wonder, then, that so many regret their choice. However, a remedy is at hand.

Whom to Call?

In some ways, estate agents are very similar to cars; different firms offer different features. Although superficially they may look similar, once you peek under the bonnet and ask more probing questions, differences emerge. Your method, therefore, is to ask several estate agents to visit your home (called a valuation or market appraisal), question them thoroughly and, based on this meeting, decide who best fulfils your needs. Your first step is to create a shortlist of companies, by researching the following:

Dominance in the Area
Drive around your area, and it will quickly become clear, from the 'For Sale' and 'Sold' boards, which companies are most popular in your neighbourhood.

Word of Mouth
Neighbours who have already dealt with agents can be useful in helping to decide who is worthy of your attention.

High Street Position
Which companies have a prime position on the high street? This should guarantee them plenty of passing trade to take an interest in your home, and so increase the number of prospective buyers.

Opening Hours
Which agents open early or close late? A 9 to 5.30 approach could miss commuters passing by the office on their way to and from work.

Advertising
Whose advertisement catches your attention in the property pages of the local newspapers? Which agents provide websites which look professional, and are easy to navigate?

Types of Estate Agents
There are two types of estate agents:

- Those owned by a large organisation, a bank or building society for example, with offices around the country

- Those that are independent, probably run by the owners, and boasting a more personal service.

Although there are pros and cons for each, it is the staff that make an office, so visit several firms, on the premise of wanting property details for a friend. Rate their level of service, presentation and sales manner.

With the answers to the above, narrow the list of possible agents to three and invite them round.

What is Required from an Estate Agent?
This might seem a strange question, as obviously an estate agent is required to

- Provide a market appraisal (suggest an asking price for your home)

- Market the property, and then

- Find a buyer at a satisfactory figure.

This, however, is only half the story. His true role is to use his knowledge and experience to

- Identify the *best* possible buyer for your home

- Negotiate an acceptable figure, and

- Manage the sale, resolving any problems that occur along the way, and reducing stress as much as possible.

These last three are services estate agents should provide, but which members of the public cannot reasonably accomplish themselves.

The Valuation
Arrange for all three agents to call on the same day, to make the comparisons easier. Each agent will want to inspect the property, and take written details to refer to later in the meeting. Use the opportunity to follow the agent around and engage him in conversation.

- How long has he been in the profession?

- How well does he know the area?

You are beginning to accumulate information to help decide how competent he is, and whether you feel comfortable with him.

The Presentation
The most important part of the meeting has been reached, the presentation. This is your visitor's opportunity to set out his

wares and persuade you to instruct him. Prepare yourself for a 15 to 20 minute 'performance', but remember the agent's purpose is to persuade you to use his services by providing positive information about his company. Your job is to prise details from him that are not so forthcoming! This is achieved by asking a series of prepared questions.

1.   MARKETING
What newspapers would be used to promote your home, and how frequently?
Local newspapers are the most common form of media advertising. There are two types; the 'free' paper that is delivered to homes, and the 'bought' paper which is available from newsagents. The latter have the advantage of being available to those moving from outside the area. Often a company will use both, to reach as wide an audience as possible.

Those with colour advertisements may be more striking than black and white ones, as well as those that use larger, more noticeable photographs.

Additional advertising?
The property sections of local newspapers often have a front page or other special feature, which highlights 'Properties of the Week'. Will the agent submit yours for consideration? They may also have their own in-house magazine which is circulated to potential buyers.

Is newspaper advertising included in the commission fee?
It is usual practice for estate agents to advertise weekly in the local newspapers and include this in their fee. However, if this is not the case and there are extra charges involved for newspaper advertising, the agent needs to declare this in his written business terms and conditions. Although unlikely for a first time seller's home, should you wish to have your property marketed somewhere not normally dealt with by the agent e.g. a glossy magazine, this too should be agreed prior to signing a contract.

2.   INTERNET
Does the agency have a website?
Few agents are without a website, providing round-the-clock advertising.

3.   PROPERTY DETAIL SHEETS
What are they like?
The printed 'detail sheet' is often the first contact a prospective
buyer will have with your home.

It is important, therefore, that it sends the right signals. Ask
to see a sample. With the advent of digital cameras, desktop
publishing and laser printing, a professional looking detail sheet
can be created easily. Internal shots enhance the look and
quality, and are a contributing factor to persuading a potential
buyer to visit your property.

4.   FOR SALE BOARDS
Will one be used?
Erecting a 'For Sale' board is highly desirable.

- It helps to locate the property; useful for night time
  viewings and properties on a main road.

- If neighbours have a friend or relative wanting to move
  into the area, a board alerts them that there is an impending sale.

A property must be exposed to as wide an audience as possible,
and few things are better than a board.

They are most effective at the start of the marketing process,
where the aim is to alert the world that your property is for sale. It
would be a pity to miss such an opportunity, especially as the board
is probably included as part of the agent's fee, and surely one of a
homeowner's goals is to 'get his money's worth' out of the agent!

Are you allowed to erect a board? This question is directed
mainly towards owners of flats who might

- Share their front garden and need permission from other
  parties in the building

- Be restricted by the the terms and conditions in the lease
  from having a board.

Always check.

5.   RECENT SIMILAR SALES
What properties has the agent sold recently in your area which are similar to your own?
The answer should confirm that

- The agent does indeed sell homes in your vicinity

- He sells your type of property. An agent that specialises in detached houses may struggle to sell a flat. He may have few of the right type of buyers on his books; he may also be inexperienced in marketing that sort of home.

6.   WHO WILL DEAL WITH THE SALE?
If someone senior is conducting the market appraisal, will he also be dealing with your sale?
If not, and you are placed in the hands of a junior member of staff:

- Will he be visiting, to have first hand information when describing your property to interested clients?

- How experienced is he? Will he have the skills needed to assist you throughout the sale? As we have already mentioned, the quality of the staff has a significant bearing on the sale of your home, and the smooth progress of the transaction.

7.   OPENING HOURS
What are the opening hours?
Estate agents normally work longer hours than most other high street businesses. 9am to 6pm is common for weekdays, 9am to 4pm on a Saturday, and some open on a Sunday.

8.   NUMBER OF HOMES FOR SALE
How many properties does the agent have for sale at any time?
Are you one of many hundreds vying for their attention and advertising space, or do they value quality over quantity and offer all clients the personal attention they deserve?

Avoid becoming just another entry on their computer database. Selling a home is a very personal experience and you want the agent to give you individual attention.

9.   MARKETING STRATEGY
How does the agent intend to use marketing to secure you a buyer?

- At what point will he review marketing progress with you?

- What happens if your home remains unsold? How will the situation be resolved?

You are embarking on a journey that only the fool-hardy would attempt without a map to guide them. Asking the agent for a marketing strategy is a good test of his experience. If he tackles the question before you ask it, this is a good sign. If he flounders and is unprepared, is he really the agent for you?

10.   ONGOING COMMITMENT
What services are provided once an offer has been made?
It is after an offer has been made that the estate agent's job takes on a new significance, by

- Knowing the appropriate questions to ask a buyer to assess the suitability of the offer

- Investigating his answers

- Negotiating a sale

- Managing the sale until its conclusion, using skill and expertise to resolve any problems along the way.

This is an agent's true role, and any that fail to realise this should be avoided.

11.   COMMISSION
What is the fee?
'Pay peanuts, get monkeys' is apt here. Choose an agent who charges a minimal amount, for example 0.5%, and don't be surprised to find that the services he provides are not as good as you may have hoped. He is unlikely to have the funds to afford decent advertising, or quality staff. Your goal is to find an agent

who will sell your home at a satisfactory price and in an acceptable timescale. This demands one with skill, and an organisation with a high level of service. These are features worth paying for.

In an effort to keep costs down, it is human nature for the first time seller to use the commission level as a deciding factor. This is short sighted. A 'cheap and cheerful' agent is not necessarily the best approach. Often a company's fees are low because this is the only way they can secure business. As a general guide, commission rates range from 1% plus VAT to 2% plus VAT for sole agency instructions, and 1.5% to 2.5% for multiple agency instructions. A good average to pay would be 1.5% plus VAT for a sole agency instruction and 2–2.5% for a multiple agency instruction.

It is also important for a homeowner to be aware of fees before instructing an agent, and under the Estate Agents Act it is the latter's responsibility to give his charges to a homeowner (in writing and prior to being instructed). Charges should be clear and any additional costs should be mentioned. This might include:

- Media advertising (as discussed earlier)

- A For Sale board (there is unlikely to be any charge for this as it is such a good advertising opportunity for the agent)

- VAT – this is likely to be on top of the main percentage fee.

Finally, discussing fees with an agent is a good opportunity to test his negotiating skills, which you will be relying on later to obtain the highest price for your home. Imagine the point in the market appraisal where the agent has just explained his fee. Because other companies are also being considered, you ask if that is the best he can do. Would he consider reducing the fee for you? The agent who immediately obliges without any argument should be avoided; he lacks competent negotiating skills. However, find one who attempts to persuade you that his level of service, knowledge and expertise warrant the fee being asked, and this bodes well for the future. He may subsequently offer a slight discount as an incentive but this is good business practice rather than commercial weakness.

12.   ACCOMPANIED VIEWINGS
Will the agent accompany those viewing your home?
Many homeowners are uncomfortable about showing strangers around their property. Apart from the matter of security, they worry about being drawn into conversations they are unprepared for, about such things as offers.

Confirm that the agent will attend every appointment. If you supply him with a front door key, ask about his arrangements for storing this safely.

13.   TYPE OF AGENCY
What are the options?
There are three common ways to employ the services of an estate agent

1.   *Sole Agency*. A single company is used to market the property. This is a popular option. The agent should show you a high degree of loyalty because you have entrusted him to be your only representative. This strengthens the relationship and ensures a better level of service.

2.   *Multiple Agency*. More than one company is asked to market your home. The fee, which is normally greater than that for sole agency, is given to the company which sells the property.

It is often presumed that this situation increases the possibility of finding a buyer. Sometimes the opposite is true. A property being marketed by several agencies may suggest to the public that either

●   The owner is desperate to sell, or

●   A single agent is unable to sell the property because there is something wrong with it.

Sending out such signals may cause prospective purchasers to view your home with caution, or put forward lower offers.

3.   *Joint Sole Agency*. Two separate agencies are employed to market the property, and work together. The agreed fee is

divided between them in an agreed proportion, regardless of who eventually sells the property. Using two agencies in differing localities widens the area of marketing, but without the disadvantages of using 'multiple agency'.

These matters should be outlined in the estate agent's contract which he will probably ask you to sign. It defines the relationship between you both, and the obligations of each party. As with all contracts, careful reading is essential. Resist the temptation to sign it immediately. It should include:

- Commission payable (plus VAT)

- When the fee is payable

- Any additional charges e.g. for photographs, For Sale board, advertising etc

- *Contract Period* – the length of the contract and the restrictions it imposes should be made clear. The period agreed needs to be long enough for the agent to market your home properly, but short enough to be able to end it if the agent is not performing satisfactorily. Four to eight weeks is reasonable. Notice may need to be given if the contract is to be terminated.

- *Asking Price* – check that the asking price quoted is the agreed figure.

- *Services* may be offered to potential buyers such as mortgage or removal services. The agent must make any services clear to the homeowner in writing prior to the buyer accepting them, as the agent potentially stands to gain financially from the acceptance of any services.

14. THE ASKING PRICE

This is one of the most important points. For most homeowners, the highlight of the market appraisal is discussing the asking price. There are two rules, however, that a homeowner breaks at his peril. Before the agent recommends an asking price, never:

- Suggest a figure yourself

- Answer the estate agent's question "So Mr Homeowner, what figure did you want for your property?"

If the agent is incapable of offering a figure without guidance from you, then he does not deserve your business.

Ask for two figures; a realistic one, and something more optimistic that can be attempted for a short period. The first is used for budgeting for the next purchase, while the second allows the property to be 'tested' on the market for a few weeks. This is long enough to gauge the public's reaction and for the owner to prove that he had attempted as high an asking price as possible. The price can then be reduced if the property doesn't sell. The danger of asking a realistic figure immediately is that you find yourself with three offers within a few days, and wonder whether you could have achieved more.

'It is easier to come down in price than it is to go up', is a good rule to remember.

This route is only possible if the homeowner is in no great hurry and the market is active. In a poorly performing market, or where a quick sale is required, asking a reasonable figure immediately is more sensible.

A Little Creativity

For properties that are a little unusual or feature a standard of decoration and fitments above average, the first time seller can try different ways to price and market the property.

- *The 'Guidance Only' technique.* Precede the asking price with the phrase 'Offers in the region of ....'. For example, imagine a flat that has been the subject of complete renovation, to an extremely high standard. It is priced at 'Offers in the region of £200,000'. Applicants with a desire to purchase something different and above average may generate great demand. The phrase 'Offers in the region of ....', has only suggested a price range. It does not limit the offers to £200,000 or lower, but allows for offers higher than £200,000. These may appear if there is healthy competition for the property.

- *Open House.* This is ideal for properties that command a great deal of interest, such as the luxury flat in our previous example. Instead of allowing people to visit your home at their convenience, limit the viewings to a two hour window on just one or two days each week. Interested parties will now have to see your home at the same time, so increasing the sense of competition. Working on the assumption that buyers always want what they can see others are interested in, this should help to secure a sale at a good figure. This method of marketing can be combined with the *'sealed bid'* technique of inviting offers. Use the 'guidance only' pricing discussed above and then request that all offers be sent to the agent's office in a sealed envelope by a certain date. This too increases the sense of competition and may result in a buyer offering more than anticipated in order to beat the others. Finally it should be mentioned that one of the disadvantages of an open house is security. Due to numerous strangers visiting the property at the same time, all valuables and items of sentimental value should be removed.

Word of Warning

Whatever techniques are used to market and price your property, you still need the agent's guidance on what amount is ultimately achievable. Be wary of an agent who only suggests one figure that seems hugely inflated. This could be an effort to impress, and obtain the instruction. While an optimistic price is flattering to the ego, an unrealistic one will leave the property unsold and the owner frustrated. Check the validity of the agent's recommendation by asking for comparable evidence of similar homes achieving such a price.

Valuing property is not an exact science and, ultimately, it's the public who determine the final selling figure. An asking price on a home is simply that – a price being asked, not necessarily its value. Finding the ideal asking price is a balancing act; it needs to be

- Realistic enough to prevent the property remaining on the market for months, but

- High enough to ensure that the vendor achieves the best price possible.

Several factors affect the price achieved. These include:

Location
I'm sure you have heard the old joke, what three things do you need to sell a property? 'Location, Location, Location.' Not particularly funny, but definitely true.

For example, if your home backs on to a railway line or is on a busy main road, then it's advisable to make an allowance for this in the price. The amount of 'allowance' will differ from area to area, and will depend on how people view the particular disadvantage. An experienced agent will be able to guide you on this.

As an aside, if someone has a need to buy your home he may disregard the railway line or main road. I sold a house beside a noisy tube line to a couple who were both hard of hearing. They fell in love with the property and the clatter of the trains didn't bother them at all.

In recent years, telecommunication masts and electricity pylons have also become factors that can affect the price of property (often dramatically) because, rightly or wrongly, health issues have been linked to these features.

Condition
The second factor affecting price is 'condition', as previously discussed on page 69.

Timescales
If you are very keen to sell as soon as possible, then ask a realistic figure to secure a quick sale but accept it only on the basis that the buyer is able to proceed immediately, within the seller's timescales, and that no further reductions in price will be considered.

Stamp Duty Land Tax
One other factor might affect the price of a property; stamp duty. The current rates and thresholds are explained on page 24; at or near the thresholds this issue now affects the amount that people are willing to offer on a property. For example, a home bought for £249,000 will have stamp duty of £2,490 (1% x £249,000) payable. However, buying a property for £255,000 greatly increases the amount of stamp duty because it is now in the 3% stamp duty bracket; £7,650 (3% x £255,000), over £5,000 difference!

This can result in an applicant making a lower offer on your home to bring it into a cheaper stamp duty bracket. A vendor whose property price sits just above one of the stamp duty thresholds has two options to counter this 'problem':

- Concede that this is an injustice but you can't buck the system. Ask a price just below the stamp duty threshold, and widen its appeal to those conscious of the extra costs involved in buying a home in the higher stamp duty bracket.

- Disregard the stamp duty factor but appreciate that a buyer might make an offer to bring it into a lower bracket.

In the past there was a small loophole, which offered the homeowner a further option. Because no stamp duty is payable on fixtures and fittings, a property could be bought for an amount that brought it into a lower stamp duty bracket. Extra money would then be given to the seller for fixtures and fittings. However, such manipulation of the system has been recognised by the Inland Revenue, who now demand that a form be completed by the buyer detailing this matter (Land Transaction Return). Questions will be asked if the amounts attributed to fixtures and fittings are unreasonable. Both you and the buyer need to check with your solicitors that the amount allocated is acceptable and justified.

8

THE APPOINTMENT

With all the preparations complete, you are now ready to throw open your doors to the public. Because this involves having strangers in your home, sensible precautions need to be taken.

It is best for the estate agent to accompany prospective buyers around your home, although this is not always possible especially after working hours. In these circumstances, the home-owner's security is of paramount importance:

- All appointments must be arranged via the estate agent, with any 'unexpected viewers' being politely directed to the agent and not given access. Keep a supply of your agent's business cards by the door to hand to these people

- Keep a note of all the arranged viewings. Record names, times, and numbers attending. During a single appointment (as opposed to an 'open house'), restrict the number of people visiting to a manageable two or three at one time. If there are more in the family, the others can call another time if necessary

- Never be alone when showing someone around your home. Ensure a friend or family member is with you

- Keep viewers in sight at all times, never turn your back and always keep a path clear to an exit

- Ensure that valuables and items of sentimental value are hidden

- Avoid appointments after 8.30 pm; there is no need to have strangers in your home any later.

Apart from security issues, here are a few tips to help enhance the viewing:

- Choose times when your home looks its best; Monday mornings after a weekend of partying, or energetic children, may not be ideal.

- Confirm with the estate agent that the viewers have full details of your home before they call. How frustrating would it be to discover after a 15 minute appointment that your visitors thought your flat was three bedroom rather than two, or £90,000 when you are actually asking £150,000!

- For evening viewings have an outside light on to help locate the property, and if possible leave a handy parking space available for your visitor.

The Viewing
One of the questions most commonly asked by homeowners is

"What do I do or say during the viewing?"

The answer is, very little. If the preparation stage has been completed thoroughly then there is no need for any slick sales patter. Instead, our aim is simply to make this a positive and enjoyable experience; one that the viewer will remember long after the event.

First impressions have the greatest influence on potential buyers. Generally, people tend to remember the beginning and end of the visit more than the middle. Use this to your advantage by guiding them towards the very best features at the start and end of the 'tour'. Leading them immediately from the front door into your flat's lounge with its panoramic views, for example, is a wonderful way to start; strolling around the communal gardens could be a memorable end. What a lasting impression this will leave! Infinitely more powerful than attempting any high powered sales technique.

This isn't to suggest we can't give matters a helping hand; a few well chosen words is all it takes. Never overwhelm the viewer with too much information, just occasionally provide details that illustrate how happy you've been in your home and how much care you've lavished on it. The visitor's bond with your home will grow, and strengthen his desire to buy. This sense of connection can be further enhanced at the end of the visit, by asking if the viewer has any questions or would like to wander round once more. I was taught very early in my career that the longer a person stays in your home, imagining living there, the greater connection he feels with it.

QUESTIONS
Be ready for the most common questions asked by viewers:

- What are your reasons for moving?

- Have you found a property to buy?

- How quickly do you want to move?

- What are the neighbourhood or local schools like?

- How far is it to the station?

I want to focus briefly on the first of these. Over the years I have dealt with people who have struggled to sell their home because of the way they answered this question.

"What are your reasons for moving?"
"Well we're not sure if we're moving yet", or
"What are your reasons for moving?"
"We're just testing the market to see what figure we can achieve for our home."

Why would anyone want to consider a business transaction with someone so undecided? This is so much better:

"What are your reasons for moving?"
"As soon as we secure a buyer on our home we'll be looking to buy one nearer to my parents."

This suggests commitment and a definite intention to move, from the type of serious minded people that can be trusted and relied on.

I am not suggesting we mislead anyone, but if a seller has a genuine desire to sell then better to describe the situation in a more positive way.

THE CLOSE

There is a tendency at the end of a viewing, when everyone is unsure what to say, for a buyer to utter the immortal phrase:

> "I'm definitely interested and I'll ring the agent with an offer."

To all first time sellers, learn from the experiences of other homeowners; until this actually happens, don't begin the celebrations.

In the heat of the moment, it's easy for a buyer to make such a promise which he later regrets (probably because he had other appointments that day and unexpectedly found a more suitable home).

So, how will you know whether viewers are genuinely interested in your home? Regardless of what is said, you probably won't. Often, the viewers who appeared least promising may buy the property, and those you thought were sure fire purchasers fade away without ever making a decision. Therefore, everyone who comes through the door must be treated as a potential purchaser. The only way to gauge their interest is if they make an offer! Otherwise the agent can call them within a day and ask for their thoughts. Obtaining this feedback will help assess how the property is faring in the market. Your estate agent can then use the results to

- Guide you on progress being made

- Implement any changes necessary to increase the prospects of securing a buyer.

So It Won't Sell

Questions to be put to the agent, when reviewing how well the marketing of the property is going, include:

- What did the viewers think of the property? Did they criticise anything that could be rectified easily?

- If a number of appointments were not kept, why?

  This could be because the property was difficult to find and better directions are needed (or a For Sale board to help locate it). Could the exterior be discouraging potential buyers from viewing internally e.g. an overgrown front garden or great difficulty parking?

- Has the asking price deterred the public? If so, is it because the property market is generally quiet or has the price proved too optimistic? This is a question to ask after 4–6 weeks of marketing.

- How many times was the property advertised in the local newspapers and what response did this bring? If poor, does the advertisement need to be written in a more 'enticing' way? Would a newspaper with a different circulation help? Perhaps better photographs are needed?

- How is the property market faring? Is it just your home that is failing to sell, or is the market generally slow?

Armed with this information, a more informed decision can be made about the future marketing of the property. I would suggest reviewing the marketing every three to four weeks.

LOWER THE PRICE?
If after several weeks the property remains unsold, this is not necessarily a major problem. It might only call for a few tweaks to resolve matters. The agent should be able to guide you, based on the above questions. The most obvious remedy, however, and often the most 'painful', is reviewing the price. Has this proved too high? If based on the agent's recommendation, why has the figure proved unpopular? Demand specific answers.

If a price reduction is appropriate, then the alteration should be handled with care. Its purpose is to attract a new group of people with different aspirations. Reducing an asking price from £130,000 to £129,000 will not achieve this. Alter it to between £120,000 and £125,000 and this may introduce it to a new selection of potential purchasers and breathe life into the marketing.

The Last Resort
If the property remains unsold at the end of the agent's contract period, here are five options:

● Terminate your business with the present agent, observing any period of notice, and choose another. Sometimes even an agent who provides a good service can struggle to sell a particular property. Once placed in the hands of another company things can suddenly 'click' and a buyer is found

● Approach the other agents who first valued your home. Ask for advice on resolving matters. Expect specific solutions rather than vague promises

● Continue with the present agency if you have faith in their eventually finding a buyer

● *Multiple agency*. If you wish to remain with your present agent, but increase your options, instruct two or more agents. However, I have always felt that this alternative smacks of desperation and sends out the wrong signals to potential buyers. If a property remains unsold then the difficulty is probably more fundamental than just the number of agents selling it. Instead, the root of the problem needs to be examined e.g. price, condition, state of the property market etc

● Choose another method of marketing while still using the services of an estate agent. Try selling privately using local newspapers, websites and a private *'For Sale'* board.

9

THE OFFER

In time, a potential buyer will appear. This is an exciting moment, as it brings us a step closer to the goal of selling our property. However, it is important not to be swept along by the momentum and overlook the offer process which is vital to ensuring success. This is the first test of how well we have chosen our estate agent. When considering an offer, the role of the agent is fundamental. He must

- Ask the right questions of potential buyers

- Use his expertise to interpret their responses correctly.

The way this is tackled will directly influence the quality of the sale. A disorganised and haphazard method will increase the chance of problems occurring, whereas a more methodical approach will diminish the danger of unexpected snags.

I hope that it is now becoming clear why so much effort was spent choosing the right estate agent. His knowledge and experience will now be used to guide us through the offer process, by accumulating as much relevant information about our prospective buyer as he can, in order to:

- Help us to make an informed decision about the buyer, and

- Continue to use this information to bring our sale to a successful conclusion.

The offer stage therefore is really where the estate agent's job begins in earnest.

THE OFFER FORM

What is our goal when someone makes us an offer? Obviously, we want to know how much he's willing to pay, although this is only half the story. Would you buy a can of paint without knowing its colour? Of course not. You'd want more information about the contents. The same applies when deciding if an offer is suitable. We need further details about the circumstances surrounding it.

1.   *Who is buying the property?*

We need to be in no doubt about exactly who the purchaser is.

2.   *Have all interested parties seen the property?*

It is vital to confirm that *all* parties involved with the purchase have viewed your home. Never rely on an offer given on someone else's behalf, except where they have written authority. For example, it is unsatisfactory for a couple to offer when only one of them has seen the property. Assurances may be given that a decision can be made on the other's behalf, but if you agree a sale on this basis you run the serious risk of the absent partner visiting your home later and deciding against it.

3.   *The Offer*

Regarding the offer itself, it is quite likely that the agent may need further guidance from you on a few points:

- Can the agent divulge to the potential buyer what price would be acceptable to you? This is useful if the property has been marketed for many months without success, and you are keen to sell.

- Can he have written authority to refuse an offer below a certain level?

- Should the agent 'play hardball' and explain to all interested parties that you want 'close to the asking price?' This may be preferable if the property is new to the market.

- Can the agent suggest to potential buyers that there may be some flexibility in the asking price?

4.   *Is a mortgage necessary?*
This is as important as the offer figure itself. With the buyer's permission, knowing his financial arrangements is the only way of really confirming his suitability as a purchaser.

If a mortgage is required, details of the mortgage lender or financial adviser are taken. Information about the deposit is also useful, such as:

- If in a savings account, is there a period of notice before the money can be withdrawn?

- If abroad, how long will it take to transfer it to the UK?

- Is it being borrowed from family and friends, and are they fully committed to this?

Most people are happy to supply such information, believing it will give their offer more credence. Those who refuse normally have a reason and we must question what this is.

Finally, if there is resistance to disclosing information regarding the deposit, (or if your buyer is wholly 'cash') then the agent might ask that the buyer's solicitor confirms the buyer's financial situation to your solicitor. If the buyer still refuses, then ask yourself why. Do you really want to do business without verifying such important information?

5.   *Timescale*
To help clarify how long the sale may take to complete, find out from the buyer:

When does he want to move?

Is he using a mortgage scheme which expires by a certain date?

Is a holiday booked which could delay the sale?

Will the purchaser wait if the owner intends to buy another property, and has yet to find one?

6.   *Property to Sell?*
If the applicant has a property to sell, or it's under offer, details are needed of the estate agent involved (or of the solicitor, if the sale is a private one). Should the prospective purchaser have no property to sell, then he will fall into one of the following categories:

- First time buyer.

- Cash buyer. The purchaser has no property to sell and does not need a loan.

- Nothing to sell. This party may own a property but will not need to sell it in order to buy yours (he may still need a mortgage). It is useful to know what he intends to do with his present home. If he plans to rent it out, for example, will he need to find a tenant before the finance company offers him a new mortgage?

WHY ALL THE QUESTIONS?

You may be surprised by the number of questions that need to be asked. Why isn't it enough to take an offer from a prospective purchaser and trust the information he gives us?

In an ideal world, it would be wonderful to be given a figure, enter into a little friendly haggling, and then settle on a satisfactory price with a shake of the hands. This approach might have been possible years ago, when business was conducted in a more civilised fashion, but follow this route today and it is an almost certain recipe for disaster and heartache. We have all heard horror stories about purchasers suddenly finding themselves short of money on the day of exchange, or unable to obtain a mortgage which they were promised was just a formality. I experienced this at my estate agency more times than I care to remember.

The sad truth is that people sometimes say things that are untrue or incorrect simply because they have been poorly advised, do not understand the system or because agents don't ask the right questions. Take the example of people who explain that they are 'cash buyers' or that their property is 'sold'. These two terms can mean different things to different people.

- Does 'sold' mean that they have found a buyer for their home or that they have already completed the transaction and moved out?

- Does 'cash' imply that they have the necessary money to buy your home, or that shares need to be sold (which may fall dramatically in value)?

I even met people who believed that they were cash buyers although they required a mortgage. It's all a matter of interpretation. Under certain circumstances, it could also be suggested that a minority seek to bend the truth when making an offer, to strengthen their position. Only by questioning a buyer can we hope to discover the truth and prevent setting in motion a sale which is doomed to failure.

EVALUATING THE OFFER
With the offer stage over, and the right questions asked, it is time to judge the suitability of our applicants. There are two considerations:

- Are the circumstances surrounding the offer satisfactory?

- Is the figure offered acceptable?

FINANCE
If your buyer requires a mortgage, he will use either an independent financial adviser or a bank/building society. If the former, then your estate agent will want to speak with him and confirm the mortgage details. This will not be possible with the latter as these institutions refuse to talk to third parties. Questions asked include:

- In the adviser's opinion, can the applicant achieve the amount of mortgage needed?

- When will the survey be undertaken?

- How long will it take for the mortgage to be issued?

- Are there any matters that might cause a delay?

- If the property requires a large amount of modernisation, have the purchasers allowed for this in their mortgage calculations (this is also a good question for the purchaser)?

It is possible that your estate agents provide mortgage services, allowing them to discover first hand the financial background of your buyer and play a leading role in this matter (within the bounds of the Data Protection Act).

Those buyers who are 'cash' should be asked if confirmation of this is possible, by providing a bank statement or asking the applicant's solicitors to confirm to your solicitor that the cash is available, in the UK, and with no delay.

SELLING POSITION

If the buyer has no property to sell, then he is worth his weight in gold. We are reliant only on him to buy our home, rather than numerous others in a chain. The word *chain* is used to describe the situation where one homeowner is selling to another, who in turn is selling to another etc., until the final buyer has no property to sell and the chain is complete.

However, if the buyer does have a property to sell, be wary of agreeing a sale until he has secured a purchaser. If he has already done this, your agent will contact the buyer's estate agent to make enquiries about his own buyer. He will discover:

- When the sale was agreed. If some time ago, is the buyer still proceeding?

- Whether the buyer's financial arrangements are satisfactory

- If the legal work is in hand

- If your purchaser's purchaser has a property to sell, and, if so, what the details are surrounding the rest of the chain.

THE PRICE

An applicant's first offer on your home is seldom his last; he is probably expecting to increase it. The success of these negotiations will depend on the agent's skill. Avoid protracted negotiations over many weeks as frustration normally sets in, and the chance of finding common ground diminishes. If a satisfactory figure cannot be agreed on, leave the 'door open' for the future. Suggest that if he decides at a later date to increase his figure, you'll be happy to discuss it (but make sure this conversation ends with the phrase 'if the property is still available!').

There are occasions where an offer is far from a homeowner's expectations. However, it may still be worthy of consideration if:

- The property has remained unsold after many months. Perhaps it has now found its true price level; a property is only worth as much as someone is willing to pay for it.

- The asking price was optimistic, and lower offers were expected.

MULTIPLE OFFERS

If there are several offers on your home, you have the option of:

- Choosing one that is superior to the rest.

- Asking the agent to return to each party and ask for their 'best and final bid' within 48 hours. This gives everyone the opportunity to increase their offer, produces a quick answer, and injects a sense of competition into the proceedings, which should help achieve the highest figure possible.

- Allowing two or more buyers to proceed, on the understanding that the first to produce a satisfactory mortgage offer will be given the chance to buy the property. A variation of this is called a 'contract race'. It works on a similar principle; every interested party proceeds with the purchase, and the first to exchange contracts secures the property. However, I must add that while these options are viable, I dislike them and feel that they are generally an unfair way to conduct business.

- Agreeing a sale with one party but on a strict timescale, e.g. he has four weeks to exchange contracts. If he is unsuccessful then there is still the possibility of the other interested parties being available.

- Asking the agent why so many bids have appeared, especially if the property has only just come to the market. It could be just a fortunate situation, which we need to take full advantage of, or maybe something has gone awry with the asking price, which perhaps should have been higher. If this is the case, it is an unpleasant situation to be in, and one which is challenging to resolve. You can either:

–   Refuse all bids. Increase the asking price of the property, and start the marketing again. In this case, it may be better to remove the property from the market for a month before remarketing, as the buying public may have already associated your home with a particular price. When a few weeks have elapsed, marketing can begin anew, hopefully appealing to new buyers who were not aware of the previous price. You may also want to change your estate agent if you have lost faith in the present company you are using. However, check the contract first as you may be committed to the agency for a certain period of time, or the agency may need to be given a period of notice before the contract is terminated.

–   Negotiate. It is possible that the parties currently interested may be prepared to pay more than the asking price. If they are keen to buy, and aware that others are also interested, then asking each party for the best bid by a certain date may help to achieve a more realistic figure.

Finally, it must be made clear that the most active time for a property new to the market is the first few weeks. Therefore, it is certainly not impossible that offers will appear during this period. Often, homeowners refuse early offers at perfectly reasonable prices, only to discover that very few more offers materialise once the initial flurry of activity begins to wane. This is not to suggest that the first offer should be accepted, or the property should not be fully marketed; far from it. We must understand how these things work and stay aware of all possibilities. If you have chosen your estate agent wisely, using the criteria discussed previously, then he will be able to advise you and resolve matters in your favour.

Agreeing a Sale
Once matters have been finalised and it is time to agree a sale there is one final question the homeowner needs to ask himself:

●   Do you propose to sell your home and buy another, or simply move out regardless?

If the latter, then the situation is simple; proceed immediately with the sale. If, though, you need to find a property to buy, then the proposed purchaser should be told. If he is content to wait, then, again, agree the sale; this will put you in a stronger bargaining position when property hunting (but don't spend any money on the sale until you find a property to buy).

10

AFTER THE SALE IS AGREED

If you had chosen a mediocre estate agent, his job would now be finished. A buyer has been found, a sale has been agreed and it is simply a matter of him waiting for his commission to roll in. But luckily, we chose an above average agent. This agent will appreciate that his knowledge and experience is about to be put to the test.

Once an offer has been agreed, there is little for the owner to do. The majority of work is now in the hands of others; solicitors, estate agents, the purchaser and the mortgage lender. There is no standard timetable when selling property. It can take four weeks, or six months. It depends on a variety of factors such as the length of the chain, the time taken to obtain a mortgage or complete the legal paperwork, desire of purchaser and owner etc. However, as a brief guide to the processes involved, this chapter presents an example of the activities which need to be undertaken during a three month sale. The first eight weeks involve preparing for an exchange of contracts (after which point both buyer and seller are legally bound), and then a further four weeks until completion (when the buyer finally takes ownership of the property).

WEEK 1

Letters
Immediately after the sale is agreed, your estate agent will send out a letter called the 'Memorandum of Sale'. This contains details of the parties involved in the sale, and the price agreed. Four copies of the Memorandum of Sale are sent out, one to the purchaser, one to the homeowner, and one to each of their solicitors.

Mortgage Forms
If your purchaser needs a mortgage, he will complete the necessary forms and usually pay for the survey, although occasionally a mortgage lender will offer a free survey. The mortgage lender may require additional paperwork from the purchaser, e.g. confirmation of pay, identification, credit check etc.

Legal Work
If this has not been prepared, the homeowner now needs to instruct his solicitor to begin the legal process. This includes:

- Preparing a contract. As discussed on page 71, the title deeds have become redundant in favour of the new Title Information Document issued by the Land Registry. From this document, a contract is created for the purchaser's solicitor, which details conditions affecting the sale.

- 'Seller's Property Information Form'. Completed by the owner, this document covers topics such as the property's boundaries, disputes with neighbours, alterations to the property, and available services e.g. gas and electricity. Owners of leasehold property complete a second form dealing with their lease and outgoing costs.

- Fixtures and fittings list. This details items to be left at the property.

Verifying the Sale
A few days after the agent sends the Memorandum of Sale, he will confirm that:

- The purchaser's financial matters have been arranged, and he has instructed his solicitor to begin working on the legal documents when received

- Any chain associated with the sale is equally well advanced.

Rather than relying on second hand information, ask your agent to speak directly to all the agents in the chain. There is no substitute for hearing things 'straight from the horse's mouth'.

WEEK 2

If the agent believes that anyone needs to be reminded again to organise any of the above, then this is the week to do it. Alternatively, it might be decided to let everyone have the chance to organise themselves without any pressure from the agent.

WEEK 3

Survey

After 7–21 days, a period which varies according to how busy the property market is, the buyer's mortgage lender will survey the property. This is arranged via the estate agent. There may be more than one survey, depending on the type chosen by the purchaser.

Little preparation is required before the surveyor arrives. Surveyors are trained to see beneath the veneer, and disregard children's toys on the floor, or clothes strewn over the bedroom. It is not necessary for the owner to be at home, although the surveyor may want to ask questions or gain access to areas of the property with the owner's help e.g. the loft, basement, outhouses etc. Lastly, don't expect the surveyor to divulge the contents of his report.

Check Progress

The agent should once again check your buyer's progress and that of the chain. If any party appears slow, then it is important to know why. Have all the surveys taken place in the chain? How is the legal work proceeding? This should then be reported back to the homeowner.

Legal Work

How far has your own legal work progressed? The two solicitors should be well under way. If a flat is being sold, are any documents needed from the company dealing with the running of the block? Having received your solicitor's legal documents, the purchaser's solicitor may have further questions, which are called 'Additional Enquiries'.

WEEK 4

This is an ideal opportunity for the homeowner and estate agent to liaise and review how the sale is progressing. Look at what has been achieved, and what is expected in the next few weeks.

WEEK 5–6

Homeowner's Position
If the owner is moving without buying another property, is rented accommodation needed? With the sale so far progressed, now is the time to start making enquiries about renting accommodation in anticipation of a successful sale (although it is still too early to give any definite commitment).

Check Sale
Your estate agent now asks:

- Whether the purchaser's mortgage has been issued and are there any conditions associated with it e.g. is it subject to additional paperwork or further inspection of the property?

- Is the survey satisfactory? If matters have arisen then this is the time to try and resolve them. This might include the need for additional surveys to ascertain the cost for such defects as damp or woodworm.

- Are there any legal matters outstanding? Can the agent help to quicken the process? It is surprising what a skilled and experienced estate agent can organise!

- Is the rest of the chain as well progressed as we are?

WEEK 6–7
With the target of an 8 week exchange looming ever closer, week 6/7 is used to contact the buyer, financial adviser, and chain to confirm their progress once more.

- The buyer will need to have his deposit arranged by now

- Any outstanding legal matters need to be reported back to the homeowner

- Any delays in the chain need to be questioned and resolved

- Have the searches been returned? (See page 54.) These are often left by the buyer's solicitors until most other matters have been satisfactorily resolved, in order to save the client's money should problems have occurred earlier in the sale.

WEEK 7
Prepare for Exchange
Before 'exchange of contracts', the following points need to be completed throughout the chain:

● All buyers have satisfactory mortgages

● All legal work is completed, including searches

● The buyers are arranging for their deposits to be given to the appropriate solicitors. These should be in the form of banker's drafts or building society cheques. Personal cheques need time to 'clear' (confirming the money is available) and so are too time consuming. It is possible that using a particular legal mechanism, each buyer will be relying on using the deposit of the buyer beneath him in the chain, via the solicitors. This is quite normal and called acting as 'agents for the vendor'

● Completion date agreed.

When all is ready, the solicitor will ask the vendor to visit his office, read the contract and ask any questions (the post can be used, but a meeting is far better for such an important event). The contract is then signed. This, however, does not yet mean the property is sold. That requires an 'exchange of contracts'.

WEEK 8
The Exchange
The exchange of contracts is the 'point of no return' in a sale. At this point, the owner becomes legally bound to sell his home to the purchaser who, in turn, is legally bound to buy it. However, there is still a remote possibility of the latter withdrawing from the sale, although the penalties are so severe that this is a very rare occurrence.

Considering how significant this stage is, the actual procedure involved is quite mundane. It takes place over the phone, and between the solicitors. I have outlined the procedure on page 64. Once finished, the homeowner can plan for his moving day, knowing that he has just one final hurdle before he has success-fully sold his home; the day of completion.

THE PROBLEM CLINIC

RESOLVING PROBLEMS

Horror stories abound of problems that occur during property sales. However, approached in the right way, so many of them are resolvable. Below are some of the more common ones I have confronted over the years.

1.   PRICE REDUCTION

A common problem for homeowners is being asked for a price reduction after a survey. It can be a testing time, but handled in the correct way, and with a skilful estate agent, stress levels can be kept to a minimum.

Firstly, decide if the request is legitimate. If due to a defect highlighted in the survey, ask to see the relevant portion of the report. If this is refused, then start to 'smell a rat'. Without proof, how can you be expected to give a reduction? If, having seen the report, however, it is a problem that could not have been foreseen, then it is reasonable for the purchaser to expect this to be reflected in the price; for example, discovering damp or woodworm. The purchaser should organise a specialist company or firm to visit and quote for the repairs. Armed with their estimate, the homeowner will then decide whether to agree to a reduction. Two points are worth considering:

- If the homeowner refuses, and the buyer withdraws, then the same issues are likely to recur with the next purchaser. Surely it's better to confront them now?

- If the amount is relatively small (i.e. £500 – £1,000), is it worth losing the sale for? That much has probably already been spent in time, effort, and possibly legal expenses.

When considering any reduction, always ask to see the final pages of the survey report. These are normally where the surveyor gives his overall impression of the property, and an opinion on the price. If this figure is the same as the one being paid by the purchaser, then plainly the surveyor believes that this is the correct price, even allowing for any repairs.

There are circumstances where the request for a price reduction is unreasonable.

- The purchaser suddenly realises that the bedrooms are smaller than he remembered

- The purchaser wants to extend the property in the future, and believes the owner should make a contribution

- The owner wants to take a set of shelves (worth the grand total of £5) and the purchaser demands compensation!

- The survey described the kitchen as dated – something blindingly obvious to anyone who visited the property.

These might seem to be ridiculous examples but I have dealt with them all over the years, and they only prove that buying and selling property brings out the worst in people. In these situations the homeowner must decide:

- How much is it worth keeping the buyer?

- Can another 'more reasonable' buyer be found quickly?

- Is the buyer still serious about buying or really just trying to find an excuse to withdraw?

2.   CHAIN BREAK
One of the disadvantages of a sale with a chain is that a successful outcome is reliant upon so many people. It only takes one party to fall by the wayside, and every other sale in the chain collapses. This can occur for a variety of reasons, most of which are out of our control, except one.

Imagine we are selling our home and buying another. There is a chain (see diagram opposite).

We have sold 40 Station Road to Mr and Mrs X, who in turn are selling their flat to a first time buyer. We are buying Miss W's house at 90 The Croft, who is moving to Rose Cottage. This is owned by Mr and Mrs P who are purchasing Mr J's home 'The Manor House'. Mr J is at the end of the chain, and will not be buying a property, as he has got another one already.

Unfortunately, Miss W's survey on Rose Cottage has not

Owner	Property	Agreed Offer
Mr J	The Manor House	£975,00
	↑	
Mr and Mrs P	Rose Cottage	£725,00
	↑	
Miss W	90 The Croft	£350,00
	↑	
Us	40 Station Road	£200,00
	↑	
Mr & Mrs X	Flat 5, College Road	£120,00
	↑	
My First Time Buyer		

been good. It highlighted some costly matters that need attention (£6,000), which Miss W had not expected, and cannot afford. She asks for this amount to be reduced from the agreed price of £725,000. The owners refuse. A stalemate is reached. Neither party will back down and it looks as if the chain will collapse for the sake of this £6,000. Where can the money be found?

The answer is, from every other party in the chain. It is in everyone's interest to try and resolve this matter. Each party has already spent much money, time, and energy on their respective transactions, which will be wasted if the sales do not proceed.

The skill of the estate agents will be needed here. They approach each party in the chain and ask for a contribution towards the £6,000 shortfall. This money can be 'passed' along the chain to Miss W by altering the agreed prices of each property. For example, the First Time Buyer may agree to pay

£500 more for Flat 5, Mr and Mrs X agree to pay an extra £500 more (i.e. an extra £1,000 in total) for 40 Station Road, and we too agree to pay an additional £500 more for Miss W's The Croft. This now gives Miss W an extra £1,500 that she did not have before. If Mr J at the top of the chain reduces the price of his home by £2,000, Mr and Mrs P can also pass this saving to Miss W. She now has £3,500 towards the £6,000 needed.

The next stage involves the estate agents. They need to reduce their commission fee to each party by £500. This too would be passed to Miss W by altering the price of each property again to allow for the fact that each party is now paying £500 less in estate agent's commission, which can be factored into the price of each home. As there are 5 agents involved, this brings us in another £2,500. Our goal of 'giving' Miss W £6,000 is achieved, at only a minimal cost to each party. Now the sale can go ahead.

This may seem an extreme example. With the price of the property Miss W is buying, would she really let the sale fall through for the sake of £6,000? I have seen it happen, and for a lot less money. 'Principle' and 'ego' can cloud people's judgments. With the cool-headedness of the others in the chain, though, these situations can often be successfully resolved. It just needs all parties to 'pull in the same direction'.

3.   NO SURVEY
If, four weeks after agreeing a sale, there is no survey by the purchaser, then questions need to be asked by your estate agent.

●   Has the survey been paid for? If not, then why not?

●   If the purchaser has not yet settled on a mortgage lender, then it is time this decision was made!

●   If the mortgage lender will not arrange a survey until certain documents have been received, can these be chased? (These documents may include wage references, past credit history, confirmation of identification etc.)

●   Have issues surfaced that concern the mortgage lender and so have delayed them arranging a survey?

This is a good example of why keeping a property on the market even after agreeing a sale is preferable. Other potential buyers can be found in case the present buyer proves too slow at, or incapable of, obtaining a mortgage.

4. NO MORTGAGE OFFER

After survey, mortgage offers should appear a week or so later. Much depends on the lender, but if after 2–3 weeks an offer has not materialised, then the agent needs to discover:

- Has the lender received all of the necessary documents in order to issue a mortgage? If not, what is missing? The agent or financial adviser should chase these immediately.

- Is the postal service to blame? If so, then can a duplicate offer be sent?

- Has a problem occurred that stops the lender from making the offer? Can the problem be resolved or will a new buyer need to be secured?

5. SLOW SOLICITORS

If the purchaser's solicitor is slow in dealing with the legal paperwork, is there a reason? While it could be because of a heavy workload, it may also be on the instructions of the purchaser. The question is why – does the buyer have a problem or some hidden agenda? Has he even instructed his solicitor to start the process, and paid him the necessary funds? This is a matter for the estate agent to investigate.

6. PURCHASERS FAILING TO RESPOND TO PHONE CALLS

On the occasions I had a sale fall through, it often started with purchasers failing to return phone calls. If a problem occurs, some purchasers follow the 'ostrich principle' and bury their heads in the sand. They refuse to discuss the matter with anyone, deciding instead to ignore all contact, even with their own solicitor. If a letter from the estate agent asking for a reply in 5 days also produces no results then presume the worst and start looking for other buyers immediately.

7. SLOW PURCHASERS

Dealing with some purchasers can be like pulling teeth. Not only are they slow in moving the process along, they need to be constantly pushed to complete every necessary task. Working on the 'Jager' principle that there is a 'reason for everything', this could be due to some concern about the purchase. If, after agreeing a sale, the purchaser is still undecided about your home, he may slow the process, hoping to find a more suitable property to buy. He may even have placed offers on several homes and is still unsure about which to pursue.

Imagine the situation of a buyer who, after agreeing a sale, takes two weeks to find a solicitor, and another two agreeing a suitable mortgage. He then takes yet another week to instruct the solicitor to proceed, and fourteen more days to pay for a survey. This is not a buyer with serious intentions. In this situation, the homeowner would definitely keep his property on the market, hoping to find a more committed buyer.

8. SLOW TO EXCHANGE

For most, reaching the exchange of contracts cannot come quickly enough. But occasionally, as this time approaches, a purchaser will suddenly announce that he cannot arrange to see his solicitor to sign the contract. Work or family commitments are common excuses. Working on the 'Jager' principle again, that there is a 'reason for everything', alarm bells should start ringing.

Ask the estate agent to confirm with the solicitor that the legal work and the mortgage offer have been arranged. Anything outstanding must be investigated immediately. This may hold the key to the purchaser's reluctance to proceed. Perhaps, for example, the mortgage offer has not yet been issued although it was promised weeks ago. Could this suggest a problem that neither you nor your estate agent were aware of? Could there be a problem with the purchaser's deposit? The agent will need to use his skills to ask the appropriate questions and unearth the truth.

PART III

BUYING AND SELLING PROPERTY: THE FINAL STEP

11

FROM EXCHANGE TO COMPLETION

One of the busiest times during a sale, for both buyer and seller, is the period between 'exchange' (exchange of contracts) and 'completion' (the moment when a purchaser takes ownership). At this point the balance of the purchase price is transferred to the vendor, via solicitors.

There is much to organise and, because most of the tasks are common to both parties, this chapter has been written with both in mind.

After Exchange

Although the estate agent's job is almost finished after exchange, there remains much for solicitor, buyer and seller to do. While the solicitor has further paperwork to complete, the buyer and seller will be preparing for a smooth move, by informing people of the big event.

WHOM TO TELL?
Who needs to know about your impending move?

- Telephone Company. Vendors should ask for the phone to be disconnected on the day of the move (and have alternative means of contact for when completion takes place). Purchasers should inform the telephone company in good time if they wish to continue with the connection.

- Utility companies (gas, electricity, water and drainage)

- Friends and family

- Milkman and newspaper shop

- Royal Mail. If post is to be redirected, there are forms to be completed. However, buyers need to check regularly with the vendors that post has not mistakenly been sent to their new address, prior to completion e.g. mortgage or insurance documents.

- Council tax

- Doctor and dentist (signing on with new ones if necessary)

- DVLA (driving licences and car registration)

- Credit card companies, banks etc

- Authorities regarding television licences, gun certificates etc

- Mobile phone companies

- Companies with whom you hold a pension, savings, shares, investments etc

- Any providers of purchases already booked, e.g. holidays

THE SOLICITOR'S ROLE

Purchaser's Solicitor
Legal documents required after 'exchange' include

- *Bankruptcy Search* – this confirms that the person receiving the mortgage is not a bankrupt

- *Requisitions on Title*. This form confirms such matters as

  - the property will be sold empty (i.e. all parties having vacated)

  - keys will be available

- how final payment is to be made for the property, and,

- how other legal documents needed for completion will be made available.

A request will be made for mortgage monies to be released on the day of completion.

Owner's Solicitor
The document that transfers ownership to the purchaser on completion is signed by the vendor.

Both solicitors will also provide a 'Completion Statement' outlining all costs involved with the conveyancing.

THE MOVING DAY
On the day of completion, once the seller has vacated the property, it is usual for his keys to be left with the estate agent (those purchasing a property privately will need to arrange collection direct). These are given to the purchaser immediately after completion has taken place. When the owner's solicitor has received the buyer's money, he will ring the estate agent and instruct him to release the keys. At this point, the seller vacates, and the buyer can move in.

Because the actual transfer of money is in the hands of others, completion can happen at almost any time during the completion day. It is possible for a purchaser to be packed and ready to move, but waiting hours for access to the new home. What can be done to quicken and smooth the process? Confirm with the mortgage lender and solicitor a few days beforehand that they are fully prepared for completion and nothing is outstanding. This should avert any last minute surprises.

Regardless of the actual time of completion, it is the seller's responsibility to be ready to vacate as soon as possible on the day. If completion takes place at 12.30 p.m., but the owners are still packing at 4.30 p.m., the purchasers will not be impressed. Who wants to move into their first home with daylight fading, and the prospect of unpacking late into the night? This is also a good reason for the seller to use a professional removal company, who are quick and efficient, rather than attempting the job himself.

If possible, the buyer should ask to inspect the property before completion. Although this may be disruptive to the owners, it is an ideal time to confirm that

● The property will be left clean and tidy

● The agreed fixtures and fittings are there

● The utility meters have been read, to ensure that the correct amount is charged to each party i.e. gas, electricity, water, etc. It is best if both the buyer and seller take their own readings.

AFTER COMPLETION
The buyer needs to

● Make the stamp duty payment to the solicitor, and ensure that he also

● Registers the property in your name, and

● Sends title deeds to mortgage lender for safe keeping.

APPENDIX I

WHEN BUYING AND SELLING GOES BAD!

However well we might have planned the buying or selling of a property, there is always the potential for problems to occur. While these might be due to the inadequate property system in this country, occasionally it may involve the companies or firms we deal with.

Unhappy with the treatment from a solicitor?

Dissatisfied with the actions of an estate agent?

Your first port of call for any problem is with the owner, manager or senior partner. It may be a matter that can be resolved by him, with the minimum of fuss. However, if this doesn't help, then the following organisations may be able to offer guidance (if the offending company is one of its members):

National Association of Estate Agents
Arbon House
21 Jury Street
Warwick
CV34 4EH
Tel: 01926 496800
www.naea.co.uk

Ombudsman for Estate Agents
This is an independent body that offers recourse to those unhappy with their treatment from an estate agent. It has the power to fine and can deal with such matters as breach of law, poor quality of service, and a range of other disputes that may arise. Unfortunately, it can only deal with estate agents who are members, and at present membership is optional.

Ombudsman for Estate Agents
Beckett House
4 Bridge Street
Salisbury
Wiltshire
SP1 2LX
Tel: 01722 333306
www.oea.co.uk

Office of Fair Trading (*Trading Standards*)
Fleetbank House
2–6 Salisbury Square
London
EC4Y 8JX
Tel: 08457 224499
www.oft.gov.uk

The Law Society
(Office for the supervision of solicitors)
Victoria Court
8 Dormer Place
Leamington Spa
Warwickshire
CV32 5AE
Tel: 01926 820082 or 0845 608 6565
Email: enquiries@lawsociety.org.uk
www.lawsoc.org.uk

Royal Institute of Chartered Surveyors
12 Great George Street
Parliament Square
London
SW1P 3AD
Tel: 0870 3331600
www.rics.org

APPENDIX II

GLOSSARY OF TERMS

Applicant Party wishing to buy a property. Also called a buyer.

Broker Another term for a financial adviser i.e. an individual who organises mortgages.

Buyer Party purchasing a property.

Chain Where a homeowner buys a property from a party who in turn is purchasing another property, this is a chain. It can be many properties long.

Commission fee Fee charged by an estate agent to the homeowner for selling a home.

Completion The end of the buying process and the moment when a purchaser takes ownership of a property (is given the keys and normally moves in).

Contract A legal document signed by both buyer and seller, prior to exchange of contracts, details information about the property being bought, and is a legal commitment that the buyer will buy, and that the seller will sell, on the completion day.

Conveyance The transfer of ownership of property or land from one party to another.

Covenant   A restriction imposed on land or property
                        (e.g. not being allowed to use your home
                        as business premises, or being restricted
                        from converting a house into apartments).

Deposit   The money needed by a purchaser to
                        bridge the gap between the price of a
                        property and the amount of the mortgage.
                        The deposit can also refer to the 10%
                        which the buyer puts down on exchange of
                        contracts (no connection with any
                        mortgage).

Easement   An entitlement to rights over someone
                        else's land (e.g. right of way).

Exchange   The moment when a purchaser is legally
                        committed to buy a property and the
                        homeowner is legally committed to sell it.

Financial Adviser   A party who arranges mortgages.

Fixtures and   Items which remain at the property when
fittings   it has been sold. Fixtures are immoveable
                        items such as kitchen cupboards or a
                        fireplace; fittings are moveable items such
                        as carpets, curtains and light fittings.

Flat   A property, often one of several properties
                        in a block reached via a communal
                        entrance.

Freehold   One of two legal methods of owning land
                        in England and Wales.

Freeholder   Owner of a block of flats, or indeed of
                        any other freehold property.

Gazump   A higher offer being accepted on a
                        property, although a sale is already
                        proceeding.

Gazunder   When the buyer demands a reduction in
                        price having already had his offer accepted
                        (but before exchange of contracts).

Ground rent	A charge paid by flat and maisonette owners to the freeholder.
Joint sole agency	Two different estate agents, working together to sell a property and dividing the fee between them.
Lease	For the purpose of this book, this term describes a document which, among other things, details the responsibilities of each property owner in a block of flats or maisonettes, and specifies the length of the lease and the charges. However, the term 'lease' is also the name of a document concerned with the rental of commercial and residential properties.
Leasehold	One of two ways of legally owning land in England and Wales. It is the exclusive possession of a property for an agreed period of time.
Maintenance charge	See service charge.
Maisonette	Similar to a flat except that it usually has its own front door, rather than a communal entrance.
Managing agent	A company employed to maintain a block of flats or maisonettes. It may be employed by the freeholder to collect service charges and ground rent, and organise the upkeep of the building.
Market appraisal	An estate agent visits a property and provides the homeowner with an asking price for the building. This is also called 'taking an instruction', or 'valuation'.
Mortgage	A loan secured on a property, normally used to buy it.

Multiple agency	Instructing more than one estate agent to market a property, but only the agent that sells it is paid.
New instruction	A property being marketed by an estate agent that has just become available.
Pulling out	Withdrawing from a purchase.
Purpose built	A building constructed for its actual purpose, e.g. a block of flats. The opposite would be a conversion, e.g. flats in what was originally a single house.
Requisitions on Title	Documents dealt with by solicitors between exchange and completion. Can include land registry and bankruptcy searches.
Residents' association	A group formed by residents in a community or block of flats with responsibility for the upkeep.
Right of way	Access over someone else's land.
Service charge	An amount paid for maintenance of the building.
Sole agency	Instructing one agent to sell a property.
Stamp duty land tax	A tax paid to the government by the purchaser of a property. The amount paid is determined by the value of the building.
Subsidence	When a building or the ground beneath it sinks to a lower level, resulting in movement of the building and causing cracks to appear. Can be caused by failing foundations.
Survey	The inspection of a property by a surveyor. Depending on the type of survey chosen, it involves examining the structure of a building, its fittings and state of repair.

Surveyor	Person employed by mortgagee and/or purchaser to look carefully at a property and advise on its condition, as well as confirming the building's suitability for a loan.
Title deeds	A document proving ownership of land or property.
Valuation (agent)	See market appraisal.
Valuation (survey)	Surveyor's opinion of property value provided on survey report.
Vendor	Party who owns a property for sale. Also known as the homeowner, or seller.
Withdraw	A homeowner or purchaser who decides not to proceed with the sale (also termed 'pulling out').

INDEX